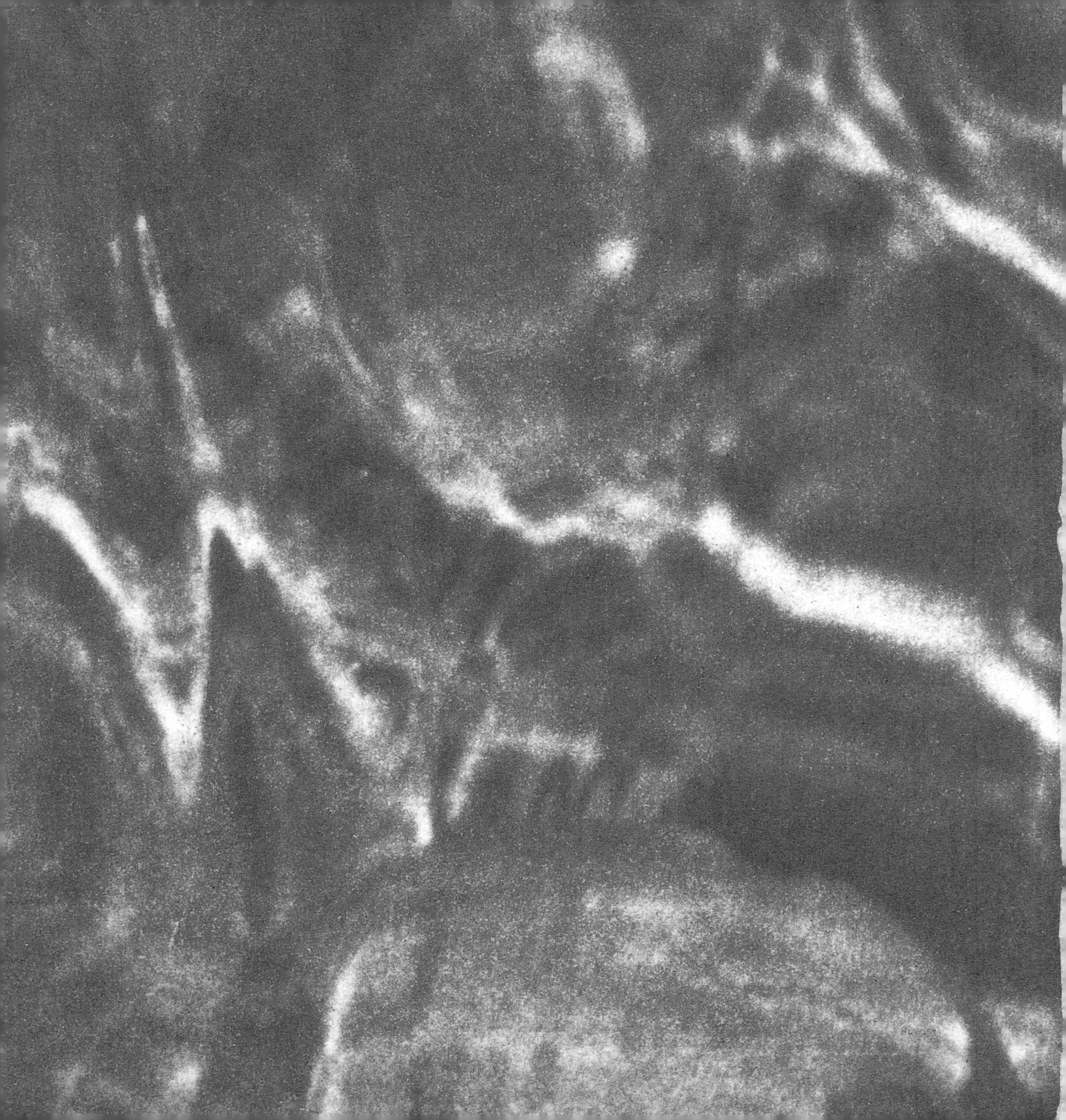

mermaids

nymphs of the sea

mermaids

nymphs of the sea

Text by Theodore Gachot

With photography by Leah Demchick

CollinsPublishersSanFrancisco

A Division of HarperCollins*Publishers*

MERMAIDS: Nymphs of the Sea

First published in 1996 by
Collins Publishers San Francisco
1160 Battery Street
San Francisco, California 94111-1213
HarperCollins Web Site: http: //www.harpercollins.com

This book was conceived and produced by
Packaged Goods Incorporated
276 Fifth Avenue, New York, New York 10001
A Quarto Company

Project Director: Elizabeth Viscott Sullivan
Editor: Nancy Fornasiero
Designers: Tanya Ross-Hughes and Anna Demchick
Art Research: Margaux King, Mariani Lefas-Tetenes, Alexander Nagel, and Emilya Naymark
Production Manager: Tatiana Ginsberg

Library of Congress Cataloging-in-Publication Data
Gachot, Theodore. 1960-
Mermaids: nymphs of the sea/Theodore Gachot; with photography by Leah Demchick.
p. cm.
Includes index.
ISBN 0-00-225038-1
1. Mermaids. I. Title
GR910.083 1996
398.45— dc20 96-13863
CIP

Color separations by Hong Kong Scanner Arts Int'l Ltd.
Printed in Hong Kong by Sing Cheong Printing Co., Ltd.

10 9 8 7 6 5 4 3 2 1

Thanks to Lisa Highton for her inspiring book idea;
to Tatiana Ginsberg and Kristen Schilo for saying the word at the
right moment; to Elizabeth Viscott Sullivan, Nancy Fornasiero,
Nichole T. Rustin, Amy Detjen, Ellen Milionis, and Marta Hallett for
their help in shaping the book; to Margaux King, Mariani Lefas-Tetenes,
Alexander Nagel, and Emilya Naymark for art research;
and to Tanya Ross-Hughes, Leah Demchick, and Anna Demchick
for making beautiful visual sense of a slippery beast.

I have heard the mermaids singing, each to each.

I do not think that they will sing to me.

I have seen them riding seaward on the waves
Combing the white hair of the waves blown back
When the wind blows the water white and black.

We have lingered in the chambers of the sea
By sea-girls wreathed with seaweed red and brown
Till human voices wake us, and we drown.

—T.S. Eliot, "The Love Song of J. Alfred Prufrock"

contents

introduction

We know very little for certain about mermaids. They slip through our fingers like a handful of minnows. It seems to be part of their ethos not to be easily understood, figured out, or explained away. They have as often seemed dangerous, lusty, and cruel as they have kind, vulnerable, and loyal. Like us, they are complex creatures, part human and part animal. Only in their case, it is more obvious.

We tend to think of mermaids as the fantasies of lonely sailors or as characters in children's books, and while those are aspects of their character and history, these creatures are also much older and much richer. Everything about mermaids is rooted in the strangeness of the natural world and rules that are not quite human. Archaeologists working with materials unearthed in the Middle East in the early part of this century were at first unable to identify a group of irregularly shaped 3,000-year-old pieces of bronze. It was only when a more detailed example was found that they realized that these crude bronze shards were actually highly stylized and heavily patinaed statues representing women with fish tails.

Images of human beings with fish tails can be traced back to the earliest periods of history. Whether or not they have ever splashed their way around the earth, as symbols they have certainly existed. And unlike many symbols that have faded and lost their usefulness over time, mermaids have been surprisingly resilient.

The character of the mermaid, as we know her today, has evolved from many different sources. The image of a human being with a fish tail seems to have appeared in cultures all over the world, from Chile to China. The fish itself is a very old symbol of creativity and abundance. Japan was supposedly created by a giant carp who, awakening from a deep sleep, churned up the sea and caused the islands to be formed. Gods or goddesses with fish tails play important roles in the creation or founding myths of many cultures. Historically, goddesses are much older than gods and were widely worshipped during prehistoric times. Because of their age, however, fewer examples of stories and art featuring these oldest goddesses have survived.

The Polynesian supreme god Vatea, whose name means "vast space," came into being when he was plucked from the side of his mother Vri-ma-te-takere, "the very beginning." He was half-human and half-fish, but was split laterally rather than horizontally like the more typical merperson. By some accounts, he is the creator of Tahiti and the Hawaiian islands and the various goddesses he seduced also gave birth to islands.

When the Hindu god Brahma inadvertently caused the world to flood by falling asleep, the god Vishnu took the form of a golden fish to rescue the Vedas (ancient sacred books) and warn Manu (man's ancestor) of the coming deluge. In this incarnation Vishnu is often pictured with the tail of a fish.

The Shawano Indians, who originally lived in Asia in a place that was cold and where food was scarce, were led to their home in North America by a man with two fish tails. This strange creature with green hair and a beard "the color of ooze" sang to them of a beautiful and abundant new land and led them across the waters to it. After safely guiding them to their new home, he disappeared.

While the fish-tailed human is the most enduring image of the relationship between the anthropomorphic god or goddess and the fish as a symbol of creativity or wisdom, the same relationship has also been expressed in other ways. The Chinese Kwan Yin, the Japanese Kwannon, and the Moslem saint Al-Khizr, "the holy one," are all pictured riding fish. Talking fish in folktales and changeable creatures like the Roane and Selkies of the British Isles, who are at times human, at times aquatic,

represent the same relationship. In a Malay poem, the father of an exceptionally beautiful girl protects her by placing her soul in a golden fish, which he then hides in a murky pond.

Water nymphs, who are lesser deities or sometimes simply spirits or sprites, have also existed in cultures around the world. Beautiful, lute-playing sea nymphs called Apsaras are found in waters from India to China. British fairies come in an incredible variety, including types associated with water and often very specific bodies of water such as bogs, marshes, streams, and puddles. Generally, water nymphs do not have fish tails; they are similar to humans in appearance.

Sometimes gods or goddesses were demoted to the level of lesser deities associated with water, but generally when there is a tail, the being represents an abstract principle such as fertility. For example, the serpent-tailed Greek river-god Achelous and the Indian Nagas are essentially sacred images of the water's fecundity. A water nymph with no tail is generally the spirit of a place.

It is out of a peculiar blending of such deities and sprites in the Mediterranean basin that mermaids, as we know them, developed. Ancient fertility goddesses in the Middle East, Greece, and North Africa were, in certain incarnations, represented as human beings with fish tails. Certain gods, such as Oannes and Ea in the Near East, were also sometimes pictured in half-fish form. Most of these goddesses and gods, after a time, shed their fish tails and were represented in human form. The images of men and women with fish tails, however, did not fade. As they spread, they were reinterpreted as lesser deities—sea gods and goddesses—best exemplified by the Greek Tritons. The Tritons were predominantly male because the imagery of fish-tailed beings that filtered into the Greek world was mostly of Near Eastern gods like Oannes and Ea rather than of the older goddesses. Tritons—along with Nereids, water nymphs without tails—were often depicted as the escorts of Aphrodite, especially in her earliest form as the goddess rising from the foamy sea. But they also established a life of their own as minor sea gods and spirits of the place.

Toward the end of antiquity, these creatures became less distinct in the popular imagination. The Nereids and Tritons, along with the Sirens, the bird women whose voices lured sailors dangerously off course, blended into a single creature combining the attributes of all three. As the Sirens' bird aspect disappeared, they were often depicted in intermediary stages with both wings and a fish tail. The single creature, a woman with a fish tail, that came out of this synthesis was more a strange animal than a goddess or nymph. By the time the rising power of the Christian church sought to discredit the pagan gods, the mermaid had safely become another animal in the medieval bestiary. Throughout the Middle Ages, animals retained many of the strange powers that had historically been associated with them, and through creatures like the mermaid, vestiges of many of the pagan gods were kept discreetly alive.

The magic of animals posed no threat to the power of the Church; instead it reinforced it by proving the presence of the Devil on earth. For the Church, mermaids were originally demon fish, unsaved souls, evil sisters of humankind living in the obscure depths of the sea. But with time they were humanized, and, strangely, the Church was in many ways the instigator of this. Theological speculation extended to the existence and nature of the mermaid's soul. The idea that mermaids did not have a soul but could gain one through marriage to a Christian gripped the imagination of both the Church and the people. The mermaid-human relationship, in its intensity and impossibility, became a resonating secular symbol for the drama of human relationships.

So it was that by medieval times the mermaid had developed into a symbol with a substantial history. She was part human, part animal, part nymph, and part goddess, with traits that were both creative and destructive.

The history of the mermaid's development as a symbol shows an unusual resilience. Over time its meaning has changed in response to the changing experience of humanity. This indicates that the mermaid is not simply a cultural or historical symbol, but also an organic one that has its basis in the human psyche. The idea of universal images common to all people can be traced back to Plato, who thought of them as the eternal Forms. Today, we think of them as archetypes: typical symbols for representing experience that are simply part of human nature. Mermaids represent tangible expressions of our feeling for the world around us, especially when that world is showing us something strange, new, or unknown. Their image is an amalgam of two parts, representing the connection between our inner feelings and our external experience of the objective world. The mermaid depicts that relationship in an image, the exact form and meaning of which changes constantly. Each mermaid's appearance and demeanor reflects a particular experience in the form of a universal symbol.

As a living symbol representing living experience, the mermaid is an intrinsic part of each of us, an image that surfaces in dreams, stories, fantasies, and sometimes in the way we interpret natural phenomena. Sightings of manatees, dugongs, and seals have undoubtedly inspired many stories about mermaids. But if these are missightings or misunderstandings, they are also rich and meaningful ones.

NOE E

CAPE

NITTING CO.

In 55 B.C., the Epicurean philosopher Lucretius offered this account of why we see mermaids:

"Let me now explain....There are a great many flimsy films from the surface of objects flying about in a great many ways in all directions. When these encounter one another in the air, they easily amalgamate, like gossamer or gold leaf. In comparison with those films that take possession of the eye and provoke sight, these are certainly of a much flimsier texture, since they penetrate through the chinks of the body and set in motion the delicate substance of the mind within and there provoke sensation. So it is that we see the composite shapes of Centaurs and Mermaids...."

He was right in a sense—subtle feelings or "films" sometimes do amalgamate in our minds. These, however, are not random images but human feelings and experiences that find natural expression in the form of an age-old symbol. Mermaids are a reminder of our connection with a wider world of which we are only a small part. It is in this role, perhaps, that they are most meaningful to us. They represent the possibility of a life outside of society and in contact with more elemental things. For some, that life has not remained only a symbol.

It is said that in 1679 fishermen pursued what they took to be a merman off the coast of Cádiz in Spain. He was an exceptionally good swimmer who continuously eluded them. After three days he was captured and taken to a Franciscan monastery. Although entirely naked, with scaly skin along his spine and no fingernails or toenails, he was otherwise a physically normal young man. For three days, despite the attentions of the monks, he did not speak. Finally he pronounced a single word, "Lierjanes." One of the monks recognized this as the name of a village a considerable distance away.

Several monks made the journey to Lierjanes with the young man. When they entered the town, he led them to the door of a house. There he was recognized by his parents as Francisco de la Vega, who had disappeared while playing near the sea four years earlier. The family assumed he had drowned. Since childhood he had always had an affinity for the sea. After returning to Lierjanes, Francisco seemed unhappy and restless, and one day he disappeared again.

A few years later, he was seen by fishermen, happily swimming and splashing about far out at sea.

The sacred fish

The oldest thread in the development of the mermaid is in the cult of the sacred fish that extends far back into prehistory to a time when the divine and the natural were the same. Fish were worshipped both as symbols of the divine and as divine in themselves. Fertility gods and fertility symbols, they were revered for their fecundity, virility, and strength. The sacred fish represented the perennial life force, continually renewing and regenerating itself.

An important aspect of fish worship was to respect the fish for allowing themselves to be eaten. This pleased the fish and ensured their fertility and abundance as a food source. But so strong was the belief in their divinity, and so important the principle they represented, that despite the importance of fish as a food source, the Syrians, to name but one culture, would not eat them. They believed that if you ate a fish, you would develop painful boils and your limbs would swell.

And if the earthly no longer knows your name, whisper to the silent earth: I'm flowing. To the flashing water say: I am.

—Rilke, "The Sonnets to Orpheus"

A sacred fish pool was created in the Ganges at Haridwar, where the river emerges from the Himalayas. The fish there were sacrosanct; for a man to lay his hands on them was punishable by death. The huge salmon swam safely among the bathers, brushing their scaly sides against swimmers' legs. In Egypt, pools with sacred fish were a feature in gardens of the wealthy. Echoes of these can be found in goldfish pools in gardens today.

Fish were also credited with great wisdom because of their close connection to the elements. An old Irish tale tells of sacred salmon inhabiting Connla's Well. A word with the fish was helpful in securing love interests and ensuring pregnancy. The fish had grown exceptionally wise by feeding on the hazelnuts that dropped from the sacred trees that grew around the well, bestowing all knowledge of the arts and sciences upon them.

Sacred fish pools were often connected to temples. Deep ponds with fish sacred to the goddess Derketo dotted the groves on the island of Delos in Greece. In *The Bestiary of Christ*, Louis Charbonneau-Lassay mentions a Buddhist library in Laos built over a pond filled with sacred fish. Sacred fish were kept in a pool adjacent to the temple of the Syrian goddess Atargatis in Hierapolis. They were bejeweled, with rings through their gills and lips and golden pendants dangling from them. The fish ate from the priests' hands when called.

Worship of the sacred fish coincided with the worship of goddesses like Atargatis who embodied the same divine principle of fertility and abundance. These goddesses were generally linked with the sea. As the womb of all things, the source of all life, the sea was considered feminine. The tides were likened to the menstrual cycle in women, both of which coincided with the cycles of the moon. The close association of creation goddesses and sacred fish was forged in this common link with the sea. They each represented the principle of fertility as the divine force that creates and ensures the daily continuation of life, and the fish came to be worshiped as an alternate form of the goddess.

At the temple at Hierapolis, the statue of Atargatis combined the two symbols into a single being. According to the myth, fish swimming in the Euphrates River happened upon an egg floating on the water's surface. Rescuing it from the reeds, they nudged it with their noses to the river's edge. Once on dry land, the egg hatched and the goddess Atargatis, a woman to the navel and a scaly fish below, rose from the newly cracked shell.

Other fertility or creation goddesses, especially around the Mediterranean basin, sprouted fish tails: the Phoenician Dekerto, Ishtar in Assyria, and Tanit in North Africa. Even Aphrodite was at times depicted as half fish. So was the goddess Eurynome, who, in one of the ancient Greek creation myths, rose from Chaos and danced on the waves after dividing the sea from the sky. The wind embraced her and she laid the World Egg, from which all things hatched.

i greet the fish of the sea respecting their ancient lineage, their swift, smooth dances, their colors that reveal other colors, their tails iridescent

like the crystal balls of fortune tellers. i lift a glass of water to all the fish still free, to their elegant, cold blood, their perfect symmetry. —Marjorie Agosin, "Fish"

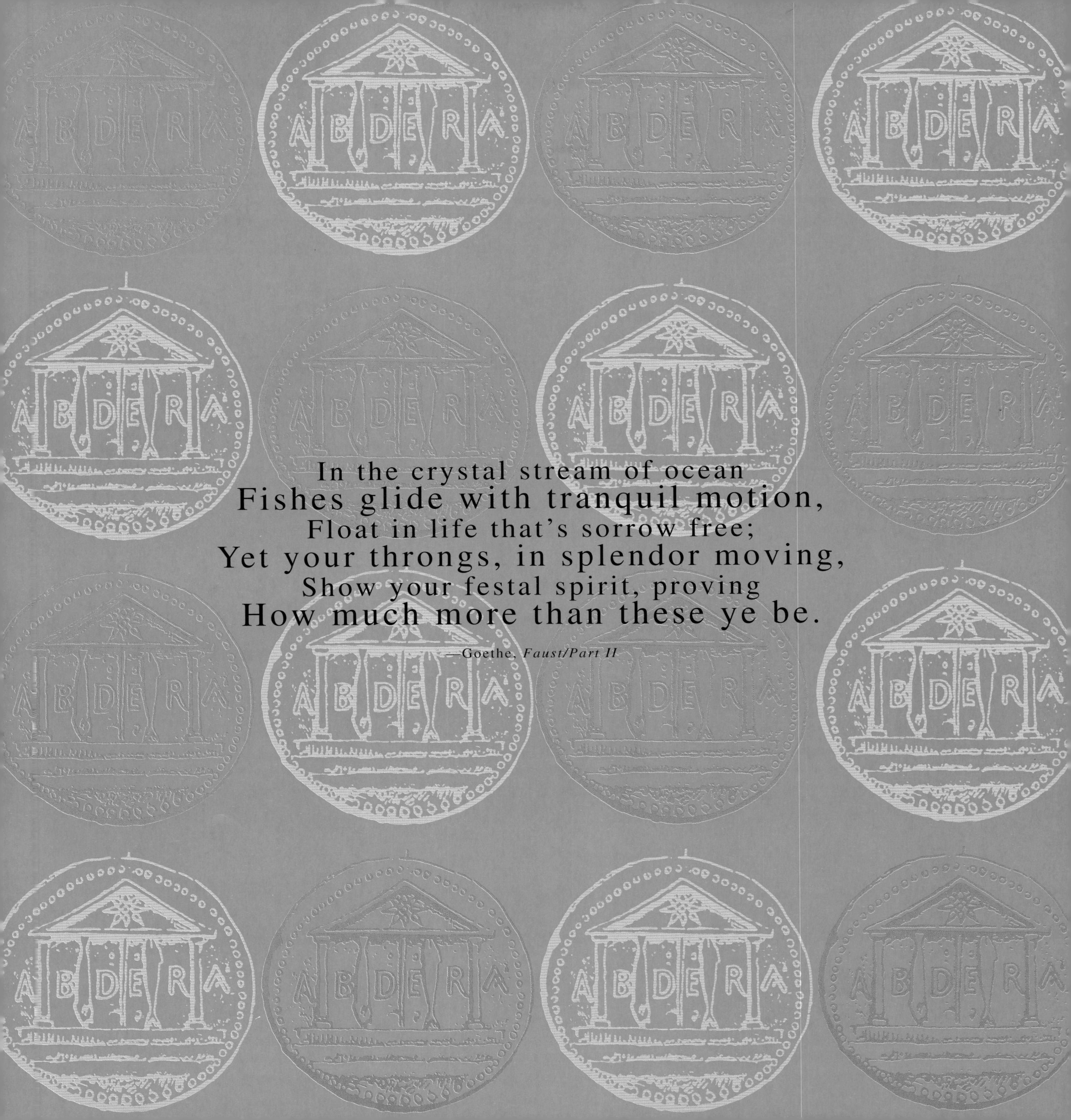

In the crystal stream of ocean
Fishes glide with tranquil motion,
Float in life that's sorrow free;
Yet your throngs, in splendor moving,
Show your festal spirit, proving
How much more than these ye be.

—Goethe, *Faust/Part II*

spirits of the place

For the ancients, the world was alive with spirits. Even cicadas, sawing in the trees, were thought to be poor souls worn to the bone by an incurable love of music. The Greeks and Romans expressed the character and qualities of certain places in the form of a *genius loci*, or "spirit of the place." These genii were usually beautiful young nymphs. They were the place's soul, embodying its character and life. Dryads could be found in trees, Alseids in groves, and Oreads in mountains. The nymphs were not only the place, but also its physical qualities and the feelings it evoked. They represented, in human form, the human relationship to it.

Nereids, the ancient Greek sea nymphs, did not have fish tails, but they are the source of some of the mermaid's most positive and human attributes. Unlike the remote fertility goddesses, they were a palpable presence, embodying the physical qualities of the water and the healthful,

teeming life of the sea. Nereids were not immortal, but according to Plutarch they lived for 9,702 years. Lithe and playful creatures, they spent their days darting among the waves like dolphins or seals, and like the sea they were beautiful, strong, and capricious.

Nereids were usually helpful to people and often acted as the guides and protectors of seafarers. In *The Voyage of Argo*, Apollonius of Rhodes described how Nereids aided the Argonauts passing through the dangerous Wandering Rocks in their search for the Golden Fleece:

"But the Nereids, passing the ship from hand to hand and side to side, kept her scudding through the air on top of the waves. It was like the game that young girls play beside a sandy beach, when they roll their skirts up to their waists on either side and toss a ball round to one another, throwing it high in the air so that it never touches the ground. Thus, though the water swirled and seethed around them, these sea-nymphs kept *Argo* from the rocks."

The Nereids' character could be tempered by the qualities of a particular spot on or near the sea. They have a specific flavor, like the spray of sea salt dried on your face. This trait was retained by the mermaid, whose appearance varies greatly from one locale to another. Some mermaids have one tail, others two; they may have feet instead of tails but be scaled all over; or like the Selkies and Roane of the British Isles, they may be seals who are able to shed their skins. Each is the spirit of the very sea, inlet, spring, or ocean from which her particular story arises, embodying the flavor of the place and of the local people's relationship to it.

Nereids were sometimes accompanied by lusty and mischievous Tritons. Triton was originally a god whose fish-tailed appearance was probably inspired by Oannes and Ea. But with time, Tritons came to be thought of as a type of sea satyr, and were considerably more wild than the Nereids.

In *The Anatomy of Melancholy*, published in 1621, Robert Burton describes a Triton up to his usual behavior:

"Peter Gillius tells wonders of a Triton in Epirus: there was a well not far from the shore, where the country wenches fetched water; the Triton, *supri causa*, would set upon them and carry them to the sea, and there drown them if they would not yield; so love tyrannizeth in dumb creatures."

Despite such fierce behavior, Tritons were usually harmless and even beneficent. They could prove a great boon to sailors, calming the sea by blowing through a conch shell.

Although basically gentle, there was a bit of the Triton in the Nereids as well. Spirits of nature, they could be selfish and not altogether attuned to the well-being of the people they admired. If attracted to a person, neither Nereids nor their freshwater counterparts, the Naiads, would

hesitate to topple a boat or draw him or her into the stream. The ancient grave marker of a five year-old girl, presumably drowned, reads, "The Naiads, charmed by her beauty, have taken the child away, not death."

According to Greek mythology, Zeus was not pleased with the chaos of nature. He preferred to rule over a creation that was a bit more regular, and set about creating a more orderly world: the Wandering Rocks should try to hold still, each tree should grow in only one place, volcanoes should erupt only so often. The Nereids, along with the other spirits of the place, didn't like this new order and quietly agreed to devote themselves, wherever possible, to overturning it by keeping alive the spirit of the particular, the singular, the extraordinary—whatever was most alive in the world—and returning creation to its original, untamed state.

The sirens' song

The sea is not merely playful or ambivalent; it can also be both dangerous and dull. This menace is represented in the story of the Sirens, whose seductive voices lured sailors to wreck their ships on the rocks.

Originally the Sirens were not beautiful nymphs or fish-tailed women, but rather squat birds with women's heads and breasts. In the original Greek myths, it was not their beauty that lured men to their doom, but the sweetness of their song. When calm, the sea lulls the senses, and when rough, it taxes them. These were twin dangers for seafarers, for their craft required great skill and concentration. The Sirens' song represented the danger of being lulled, distracted from the task at hand. The danger was in this loss of attention, a lapse in the concentration necessary to navigate the rough seas, and the constant need to sublimate instinct and remain in control. The danger was not in falling in love, but rather in being enraptured and losing consciousness.

The word *siren* literally means "entangler," and the beauty of her song is the beauty of the elements and the pull of instinct. No one could sail safely past the Sirens. According to Greek mythology, only two men ever had, and it is interesting how they managed. Odysseus, known for his craftiness, was lashed to the mast of his ship; and Orpheus beat the Sirens by practicing his craft, music, and drowning out their voices by playing a song more beautiful than theirs. The song of the Sirens was so powerful that Odysseus' crew had to stuff their ears with beeswax so as not to fall prey to their charms, and on Orpheus' ship even his masterful lyre playing could not completely drown out the Sirens' song—the crewman Butes threw himself madly from the deck of the *Argo* to be with the squat birds.

There are several stories of the Sirens' origins. They were probably originally water nymphs, the daughters of Achelous, a river god, or Phorcys, one of the old men of the sea. They became birds when a goddess or witch, jealous and angry, enchanted them. Water nymphs embody the qualities of the sea, and an enchanted water nymph, appropriately, embodies the qualities of the sea gone mad.

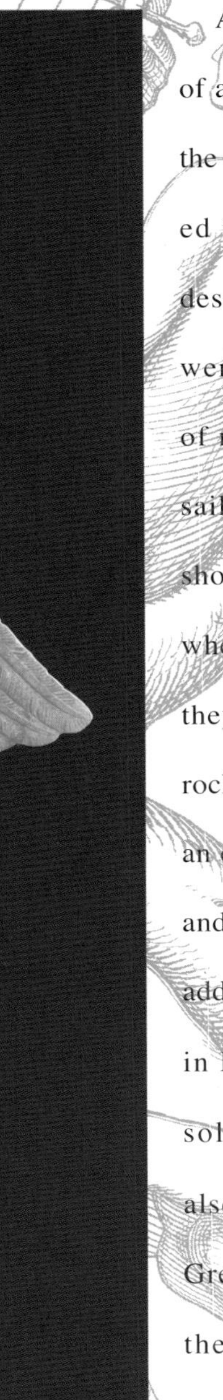

Aldrovandris, the author of a medieval bestiary, thinks the story might have originated in sailors who, after the desolation of a long voyage, were attracted by the sound of nightingales singing and sailed too close to the rocky shores of the Mediterranean, where—especially at night—they would be dashed on the rocks. Male nightingales have an especially melodious song, and there might have been an added impetus in the fact that in Rome the birds could be sold for large sums. It has also been suggested that the Greeks invented the story of the Sirens to frighten their commercial competitors.

The Siren's transformation from bird to fish-tailed nymph can be traced in the text and illustrations of medieval bestiaries. The following description is from a famous bestiary known as the *Physiologus*:

"They give forth musical songs in the melodious manner, which songs are very lovely, and thus they charm the ears of sailormen and allure them to themselves. They entice the hearing of these poor chaps by a wonderful sweetness of rhythm, and put them to sleep. At last when they see the sailors are deeply slumbering, they pounce upon them and tear them to bits. That's the way in which ignorant and incautious human beings get tricked by pretty voices, when they are charmed by indelicacies, ostentations and pleasures, or when they become licentious with comedies, tragedies and various ditties. They lose their whole mental vigor as if in a deep sleep, and suddenly the reaving pounce of the enemy is upon them."

As her legend developed, the deadly Siren worked on unsuspecting men less through their ears than through certain other senses, contributing an indelible facet to the mermaid's character.

In a medieval story from the British Isles, a certain Lord Lorntie, out for a ride with his servant, had his attention diverted by the screams of a beautiful woman afloat at the edge of a lake. Believing her to be in imminent danger of drowning, Lorntie went quickly to the water's edge and was about to jump in when he was grabbed from behind by his man. Shocked that his servant would interfere, he was tempted to hit the man when the woman dove, revealing a glimmering fish tail. The two quickly returned to their horses, but the mermaid resurfaced and in a devilish cooing voice sang: "Lorntie, Lorntie were it not for your man, I had gart your hart's bluid skirl in my pan."

He's taken her by the milk-white hand, And he's thrown her in the main;

And full five-and-twenty hundred ships

Sank all on the coast of Spain.

—Anonymous, "The Daemon Lover"

But she, with astounding vigor, emerged straight from the sea as far as the waist and put her arms around my neck, enveloping me in a scent I had never smelled before, then let herself slither into the boat: beneath her groin, beneath her gluteal muscles, her body was that of a fish, covered in minute scales of blue and mother-of-pearl, and ending in a forked tail which was slowly beating the bottom of the boat. She was a mermaid.

—Giuseppe di Lampedusa, "The Professor and the Mermaid"

moon and mirror

Mermaids are often seen in the moonlight, perched on craggy rocks in the surf, combing their hair as they gaze into a mirror. The mirror and comb first appeared in their hands during late Roman times, when mermaids began to be thought of as "real" creatures, almost human, but with a strong aura of the magic of animals.

Although their origin is uncertain, the mirror and comb may have developed out of misreadings of the various objects held by some of the early proto-mermaids. Sirens were occasionally depicted holding harps or lyres to accompany their singing. The comb may be a misinterpretation of those instruments—the arching back of the harp became the spine of the comb and the strings, the teeth. Also, Nereids were sometimes shown holding fish, and the stylized representation of spines in the fish's fins may have been mistaken for the teeth of a comb.

Aphrodite was sometimes pictured on coins holding a scallop shell in one hand and a sea anemone in the other. Both of these objects are fertility symbols and represent the goddess' relationship to the sea. It is possible that the tiny images on the coins were misread. The round shell held up next to Aphrodite's face may have been seen as a mirror, and the tentacles of the anemone she grasped in her other hand as the teeth of a comb. This association is likely since mirrors figure in several myths featuring Aphrodite. Complicating matters further, *kteis*, the Greek word for "comb," is also the word for "scallop shell."

But the play on the meaning of *kteis* might have been more self-conscious. *Kteis* and the Latin word for comb, *pecten*, can also mean "vulva." The comb may have been purposefully chosen to represent the mermaid's emerging sexuality. While the older fish-tailed goddesses represented fertility as a divine principle, the mermaid—part human and part animal—came to represent the corporeal nature of sexuality.

The mirror is rich with associations to mermaids. Its polished silver surface is reflective like the surface of the sea. Its round shape and luminescence connect it with the orb of the moon. And the moon controls the sea, the womb of all things. Both the moon and the mirror, because of their color and shape, were connected with the image of the World Egg, from which the world and everything in it were hatched.

As the character of the mermaid developed, the mirror and comb were most frequently interpreted as emblems of her vanity and selfishness. But there is an interesting twist on the theme of the mirror: It is said that a person looking into a mermaid's mirror can see his or her true self. This is just one of the mermaid's many unusual powers. In ancient times, people were fascinated by the question of the source of this power, and were especially curious about the Sirens' song. There was much debate about why this song was so powerfully alluring: What words and notes were uttered that could possess men so completely? Pondering this question, the famous Roman orator Cicero decided: "Homer could see that this fable would be without value if the Sirens sang nothing but little songs to catch a man like Ulysses in their net: It is, then, knowledge that the Sirens promise."

Mermaids do have a strange sort of knowledge that is apparent in their skill with prophecy. They are able to predict and control storms at sea, and they can also foretell events. A well-known example is the mermaid named Isbrandt who predicted the birth of King Christian IV to a Danish fisherman. In many encounters mermaids make incomprehensible sounds or say things that are difficult to understand. These words were thought to have strange meanings, much like the enigmatic utterances of the ancient oracle at Delphi. The oracle made her pronouncements in a state of inspired trance, and over her doorway were inscribed the words "know thyself."

The symbolic meanings of the mirror and comb point away from the mermaid's vanity and toward moonlight on the surface of the water. Plato praised the irrational when it took the form of oracular wisdom, prophecy, or frenzy. Like the mesmerizing dance of light on water, the mermaid's wisdom is divine lunacy. What she knows, she knows from experience; wind-tossed, salt-sprayed, supple, and visceral, she gains her knowledge from contact with life, from rolling in it, like a crashing wave.

Who would be
A mermaid fair,
Singing alone,
Combing her hair
Under the sea
In a golden curl
With a comb of pearl
On a throne?

—Alfred, Lord Tennyson, "The Mermaid"

STERLING 300-42

STERLING 300-42

The mermaid's soul

During the Middle Ages, the mermaid as we know her today flourished in the popular imagination, and the Church played a surprisingly active role in her promotion. While the Church had sought to discredit the majority of the pagan deities, it kept the mermaid as a symbol of licentiousness and as a reminder of the perils the temptations of the flesh posed to the immortal soul. Depicted with a look of devilish willingness and a divided tail to emphasize her concupiscence, and preening herself with a mirror and a comb, the mermaid was frequently used as an emblem in churches and cathedrals. The idea of employing the mermaid as such a symbol worked a little too well, though—her somewhat lascivious image proved to be quite distracting for otherwise devout individuals, conjuring up forbidden pleasures and adding to the mermaid's popularity.

The mermaid, however, served the Church as more than a mere emblem. The abundance of mermaid sightings supported the Church's belief in an orderly universe where, just as man was created in the image of God, the forms of life on earth were thought to be paralleled in the sea. Men and women walked the earth, so it was simple symmetry that mermen and mermaids swam in the seas. After all, there were sea horses whose resemblance to terrestrial horses was beyond question, and what were eels if not aquatic snakes? The symmetry was steadfastly believed as this excerpt from *Divine Weekes & Works*, a bestiary compiled by Guillaume de Saluste Du Bartas in 1558, attests:

"Seas have...Rams, Calfs, Horses, Hares and Hogs,
Wolves, Lions, Urchins, Elephants and Dogs,
Yea, Men and Mayds; and (which I more admire)
The Mytred Bishop, and the Cowled Fryer:
Whereof examples (but a few years since)
Were shew'n the Norway's and Polonian Prince."

According to Gisbertus Germannus and a number of other sources, a monk fish was found on the coast of Norway in 1531, and a bishop fish was caught off the coast of Poland at about the same time. The monk was taken to Copenhagen, but did not live. The bishop, however, was taken for an audience with the King of Poland. Though unable to speak, the bishop made clear his desire to continue his work in the sea and was allowed to do so. The English author T. H. White in the appendix to *The Book of Beasts*, a Latin bestiary he translated, explains: "His Grace was not happy in Poland and after pleading for his liberty with the assembled clergy by means of signs, was reverently returned to his native element. Perhaps he was a walrus because some Bishops have looked like decayed walruses, but the matter is now beyond conjecture."

The existence of these fish was taken seriously by some naturalists as late as the seventeenth century. One real bishop, Erik Pontoppidan of Norway, who was also the author of *A Natural History of Norway*, was a staunch supporter of the existence of mermaids. Although he was certain that mermaids and mermen existed, he also believed that many of the reports and stories connected to them were exaggerated or simply false: "Whilst we have no ground to believe all these fables, yet as to the existence of the creature we may safely give our assent to it."

The fish was an important image for the early Christians; it was used as a secret symbol for Christ by those fearing Roman persecution. These Christians discovered that the first letters of the Greek words for "Jesus Christ, God's son, Savior," spelled the Greek word for fish, *ichthys*. Because the beginning of the Christian era coincided with the start of the astrological age of Pisces, the two fish in the constellation were interpreted as Christ and Antichrist. The northern fish was Christ, and the southern fish, facing the opposite direction, was often symbolized by the merman, mermaid, or devil fish.

One mermaid, whose name was Liban, was captured in northern Wales around the sixth century A.D. She was taken to a church and kept in a barrel of water. The clergy baptized her Murgen, meaning "sea born," and gave her a choice: she could live out the expected mermaid life span of three hundred years or she could die and go directly to heaven. She chose death, and because of her martyrdom became a saint. A number of miracles have been ascribed to her.

Mermaids were occasionally encountered by priests strolling by the seaside or taking walks near lakes in the woods. Upon meeting the demon fish, the priests would curse them as devils and shower them with threats of eternal damnation. The mermaids' usual response was to break into tears. (A mermaid on the Isle of Iona was so upset by these condemnations that she made daily visits to a holy man living there to plead for a soul. Her tears turned into the unusual greenish pebbles that can be found there today.) Eventually, the tears of the mermaids softened the priests' hearts. They began to wonder whether they should be tending to the mermaids' souls, rather than cursing them. A feeling of kinship with our aquatic cousins began to develop. Emerging reports of mermaids being eaten in parts of Africa sharpened the debate over their souls—if mermaids had souls, then this custom amounted to cannibalism. Eventually it was decided that mermaids did not have souls, but they could be granted them through marriage to a Christian.

A relatively recent example of the Church's fascination with mermaids can be found in Robert Hawkes, who in 1826 was soon to become the vicar of Morwenstow. In July of that year, for some reason and for several nights in a row, Hawkes secretly dressed as a mermaid and positioned himself on a rock in the shallow water. There, holding a mirror, he sang loud songs and splashed about under the moon, until he was found out.

For the cold strange eyes of a little Mermaiden

And the gleam of her golden hair.

. . . We shall see, while above us

The waves roar and whirl,

A ceiling of amber, A pavement of pearl.

—Matthew Arnold, "The Forsaken Merman"

The seven seas

The great age of mermaid and merman sightings was ushered in by the Roman naturalist Pliny in A.D. 77, when he reported in his *Natural History* strange goings-on off the coasts of Portugal and Spain. "I have illustrious knights as authority for the assertion that a Triton has been seen by them in the Gulf of Gades, perfectly resembling a man in his physical appearance. They say that he climbs aboard ships during the night, and that the side of the ship on which he sits is weighed down, and if he should happen to stay an unduly long time, the ship is submerged."

About a hundred years later, Pausanias, ancient inventor of the travel guide, described a Triton preserved in honey at Tanagra in Boeotia, Greece, and another he had seen in Rome. "Tritons are certainly a sight; the hair on their heads is like the frog's in stagnant water: not only in its froggy color, but so sleek you could never separate one hair from the next: and the rest of their bodies are bristling with very fine scales like a rough-skinned shark. They have gills behind the ears and a human nose, but a very big mouth and the teeth of a wild beast. I thought the eyes were greenish-gray, and they have their hands and fingers and fingernails crusted like sea-shells. From the breast and belly down they have a dolphin's tail instead of feet."

Damostratos, author of a work on sea monsters, studied the Triton at Tangara to determine its authenticity. Burning a piece, he was able to conclude only that it stank, but not in a fishy way.

According to a local legend, the Blue Men of Minch were a peculiar group of mermen who would attack boats in the Hebrides. Strangely sensitive to language, they were terribly confused if you spoke to them in rhyme and were rendered helpless if you had the last word or could sing better than they. Some fishermen discovered one asleep on the surface of the water, bound him, and took him into their boat. Two more Blue Men followed, swimming behind the boat. One said, "Duncan will be one," the other replied, "Farquahar will be two," after which the prisoner suddenly snapped out of his ropes and swam away.

In the eighteenth century, a mermaid was captured by fishermen on the Isle of Man and kept for three days. Upon being released, she could only comment that human beings are so ignorant that they throw out the water in which they've boiled eggs. Another caught later in the same region was asked about the properties of water in which eggs had been boiled. She replied, "If I tell you that, then you would have a tale to tell."

Seven mermen and mermaids were beached at Manaar, west of Sri Lanka, in 1560. Their bodies were taken to Goa, India, where Demas Bosquez, physician to the Portuguese viceroy, dissected them and found their internal structure to be exactly like that of human beings.

Another mermaid was discovered live in 1727 near Amboina in Indonesia and was presented to the Dutch governor. François Valentijn, a colonial chaplain, described her in his *Natural History of Amboina*. "What do they say to the fact that in 1712 a mermaid was not only seen but captured near the island of Borneo, five feet, Rhineland measure, in height; which lived four days and seven hours, but refusing all food died without leaving any intelligible account of herself?"

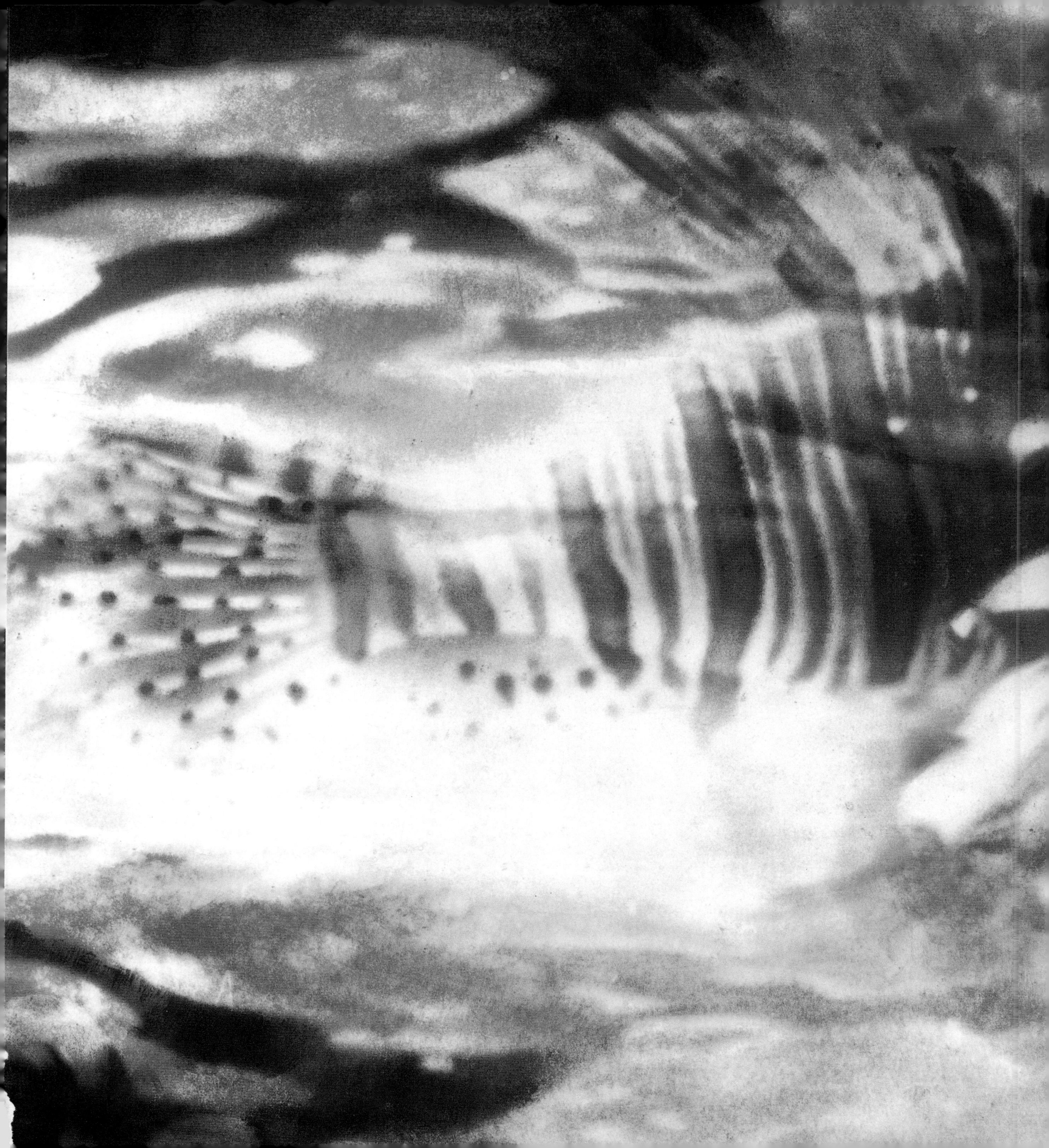

In my childhood rumours ran
Of a world beyond the door—
Terrors to the life of man
That the highroad held in store.

Of the mermaids' doleful game
In deep water I heard tell,
Of lofty dragons puffing flame,
Of the hornèd fiend of Hell.

—Robert Graves, "Mermaid, Dragon, Fiend"

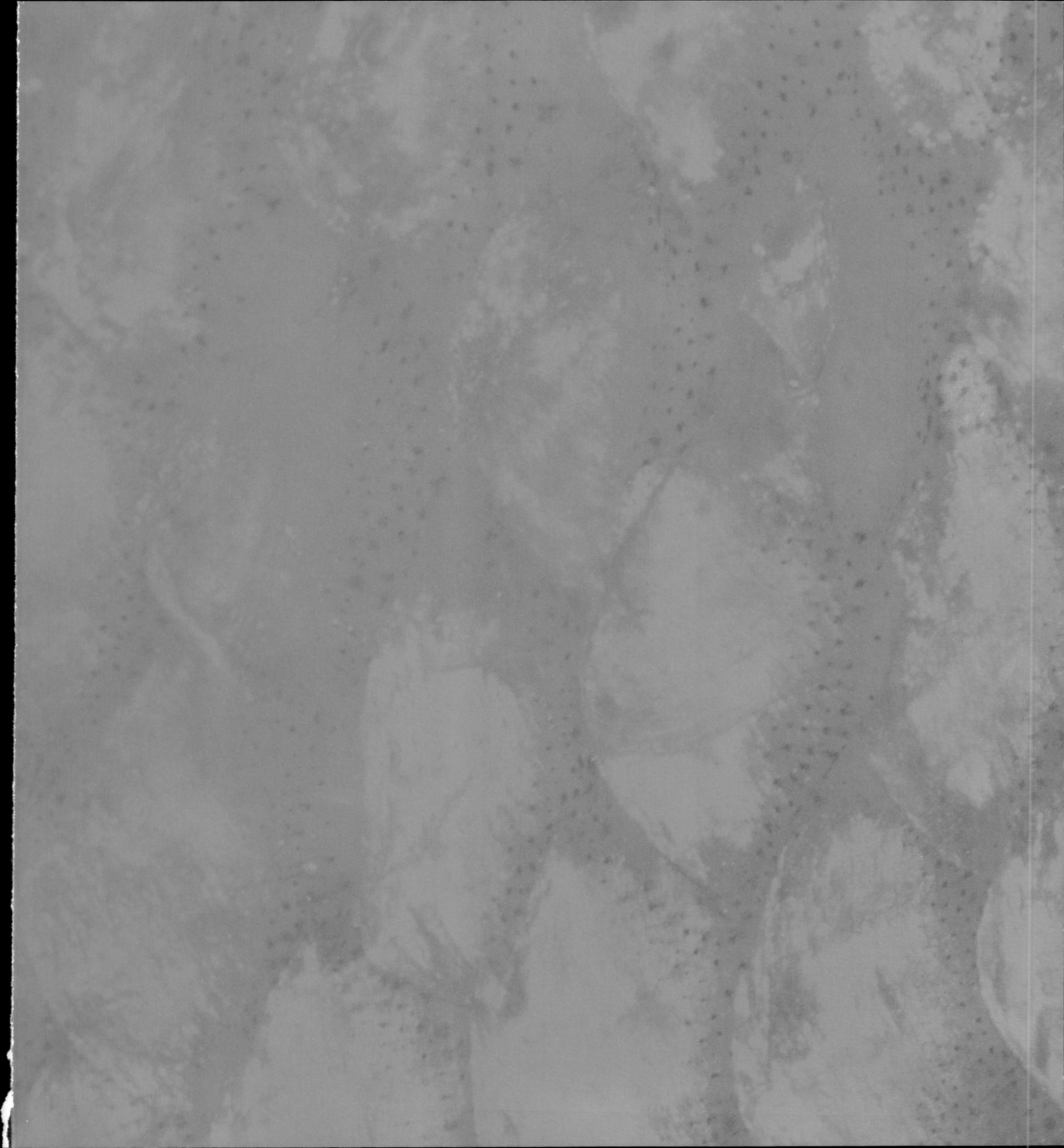

I started Early—Took my Dog—

And visited the Sea—

The Mermaids in the Basement

Came out to look at me....

—Emily Dickinson, "I Started Early—Took My Dog"

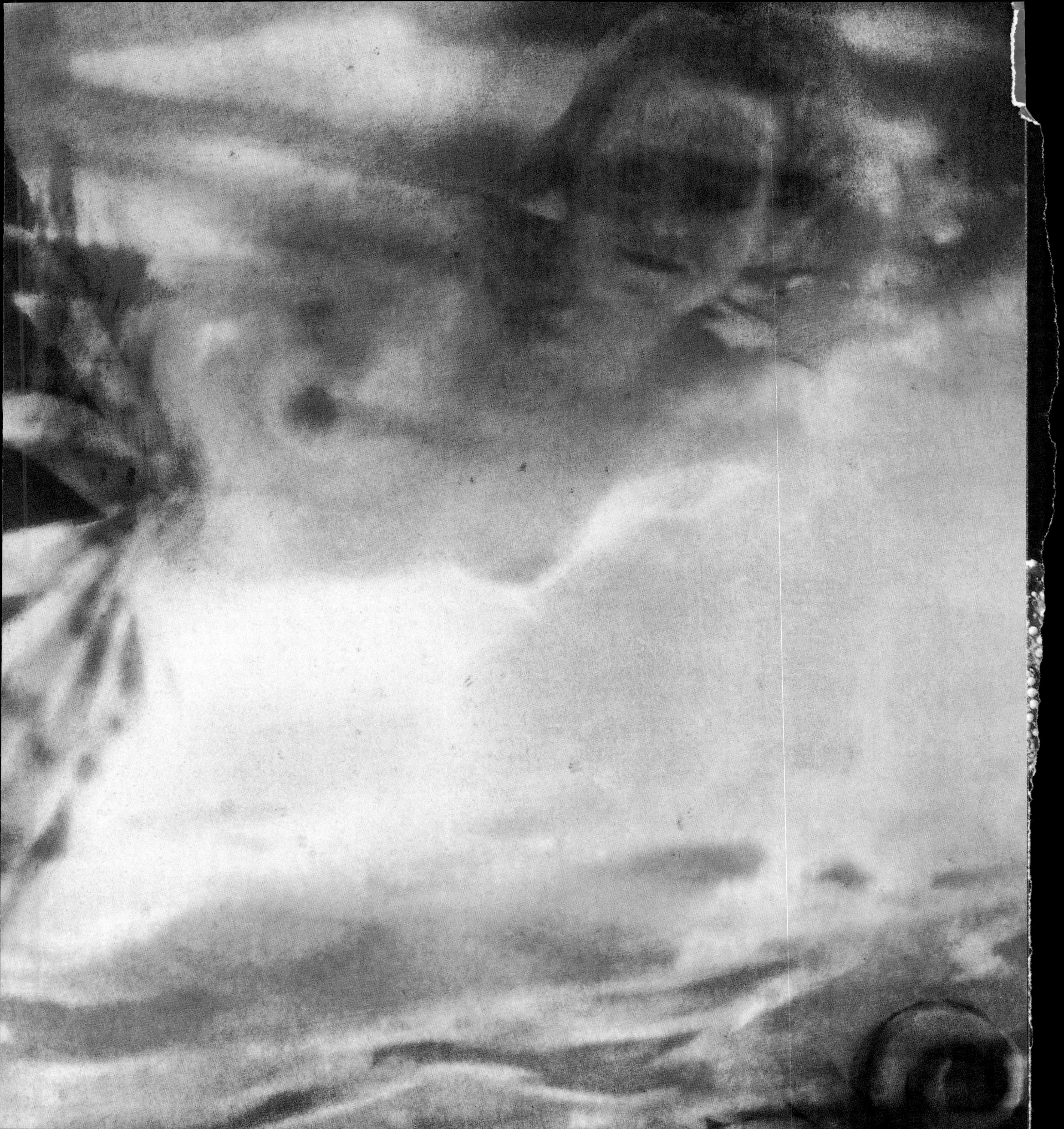

Throughout the Middle Ages, mermaids and mermen were repeatedly sighted in Scandinavian waters. A merman captured near Bergen in Norway was brought before King Hiorleif to sing. The merman, it turned out, had a terrible voice. He was put in a bathtub, in which he dissolved overnight. The water was, incidentally, thrown out. Another merman caught by two Danish senators threatened, in fluent Danish, to sink their ship if he was not released.

Christopher Columbus recorded in a log entry of January 9, 1493, made near the island of Hispaniola, "I saw three sirens that came up very high out of the sea. They are not as beautiful as they are painted, since in some ways they have a face like a man."

Brazilian mermen were so vicious, according to *A Treatise of Brasil* (1601), that it was fatal even to think of them. We have from witnesses—"two reputedly sober and dependable observers, the Jesuit father Fernao Cardim and the sugar manufacturer Gabriel Soares de Sousa"—that mermen, after strangling and crushing their victim, would either "let out curious sighs" or dine on the "eyes, nose, finger and toe tips" as well as other select parts.

In the early seventeenth century, two members of the English navigator Henry Hudson's crew saw a mermaid in the Arctic waters off Novaya Zemlya. "From the navel upward her back and breasts were like a woman's, as they say that saw her; her body as big as one of ours; her skin very white, and long hair hanging down behind, of colour black. In her going down they saw her tail, which was like the tail of a porpoise and speckled like a mackerel."

Captain Sir Richard Whitbourne, the "Devon sea-dog," in his *Discourse and Discovery of New-found-land* (1620), records a "strange creature" resembling a beautiful woman with a tail "something like a broad hooked arrow" that tried to board a small boat. The crew "struck it a full blow on the head, whereby it fell off from them." Whitbourne concludes, "This I suppose was a Mermaid or Merman."

Around 1723, a Danish Royal Commission was formed to investigate the spate of local mermaid sightings. If the Commission found that mermaids did not exist, it would be against the law even to mention them. After some days with no luck, the Commission happened upon what seemed to be a log floating in the sea off the Faeroe Islands. The "log" proved to be a merman with deep-set eyes who stared them down for several minutes. When the Commission became officially frightened and started to pull away, the merman let out an extremely loud bellow and disappeared into the ocean.

The Richmond Dispatch, in July 1881, reported the story of a woman who, fearing for her life at the hands of someone in Cuba, jumped into the sea. She was apparently rescued by mermaids who placed her safely on a ship headed for New Orleans.

As the world became more well known, the number of mermaid sightings declined hand in hand with the spirit of seafaring adventure. In the 1920s the Romanian poet Tristan Tzara summed up the ensuing boredom: "I would have been an adventurer with grand gestures if I could have accomplished one thing: not to be bored."

romance and magic

"One should have more respect," the philosopher Nietzsche wrote, "for the bashfulness with which nature has hidden behind riddles and iridescent uncertainties. Perhaps truth is a woman who has reasons for not letting us see her reasons."

Most mermaid marriages are troubled by a single problem: Mermaids cannot live in a purely human world; they are inevitably drawn back into the waters. In a common scenario, a man gains power over a mermaid by possessing her cap, cloak, or seal's skin (if she is a Selkie or Roane). As long as he keeps the object, the mermaid stays. She usually becomes a loving wife and a good, caring mother, but if she happens to find her cap or skin she can't help herself—no matter how much she may love her husband and family, the call of the sea is stronger and she must return to her original home.

In tales of human-mermaid romance, the need to return to the water became an emblem of the distance between the sexes that could be bridged only through the cultivation of empathy. The mermaid's appearance was proof of the possibility of such empathy—the relationship of two disparate parts working as a whole.

A small act of empathy and respect, unusual in human-mermaid relations, was recorded by Alexander ab Alexandro in 1552. A mermaid, a beautiful woman to the belly and a fish below, washed ashore on a beach in Greece. A crowd formed to gawk at the strange sight. The mermaid, upset by this attention and the people who hemmed her in, began to cry. Seeing this, Theodore de Gaza carried the thankful mermaid to the water, where she quickly disappeared below the waves. She resurfaced a few moments later, uttered some incomprehensible words, and was seen no more.

For recognizing the mermaid's need to return to her element, de Gaza received her heartfelt, if unintelligible, gratitude. But respecting a mermaid's freedom could also be the source of incredible rewards. A mermaid found by a Scottish fisherman offered him a wish in exchange for returning her to the sea. He agreed and asked for a boat that would never sink and from which no man would ever be lost. The mermaid built the boat with her own hands, and according to the legend the wish held true.

In the medieval French story of Melusine, Raymond, a count, meets a strange and beautiful woman by a fountain in the forest. This woman, Melusine, suggests that they get married. But there is one condition: She must be alone every Saturday, and Raymond must not ask why. He agrees, and Melusine builds a beautiful chateau for them to live in. All goes well, and in a short time they have many children.

A mermaid found a swimming lad, picked him for her own,

The children are a little strange—each in its own way resembling an animal—but they grow up to be unusually talented in particular crafts, which more than compensates for their appearances.

One fateful day, having overheard some gossips discussing his wife's need to be alone on Saturday, Raymond grows jealous and suspicious. The next Saturday he peeks into her room, half-expecting to find her in the company of another man, and is surprised instead to see Melusine splashing about in her bath. Where before she had long, pale legs, she now has a powerful fish tail. Raymond, both troubled and relieved, says nothing to Melusine, as he fears the consequences of breaking their pact. But in time there is trouble with the children: In a fight, one brother kills another. Raymond, beside himself with despair, can think only of Melusine's tail as the source of his children's beastliness. In a rage, he blames her. When Melusine understands that Raymond has broken his vow, she has no choice. She flees without a word, via one of the windows of the chateau, leaving only a mark in the shape of a single footprint where she last stood.

Mermaids can offer boons if respected and deliver evils if not. They can cause or prevent storms, bring treasure from the bottom of the sea, cause ruin, cure illness, or bring about death. Melusine is credited with building castles and erecting monuments in Brittany that still exist today. Several notable families claim her as their ancestor, and she is said to return at the death of each family member.

In most folktales and legends, marriages on mermaid's terms are seen as death to those who accept. But nonetheless many have gone gladly. A story from Cornwall, England, soberly recalls that Matthew Trewella sang in a church choir and that a mermaid would come to the church every day and sit quietly in a pew listening. She fell in love with his voice and, in time, with him. One day she invited him to follow her into the sea and he did so gladly. The people of the village assumed that this was his end. But a few years later, a mermaid boarded a boat and asked the skipper if he could move his anchor. It was blocking the door to her house, and she was anxious to get home to see her husband, Matthew Trewella, and their children.

pressed her body to his body, Laughed; and plunging down Forgot in cruel happiness That even lovers drown. —W.B. Yeats, "The Mermaid"

Once I sat upon a promontory,
And heard a mermaid on a dolphin's back
Uttering such dulcet and harmonious breath,
That the rude sea grew civil at her song,
And certain stars shot madly from their spheres
To hear the sea-maid's music.

—William Shakespeare, *A Midsummer Night's Dream*

sideshow

Nympholepsy, a sort of madness brought on by extended contact with nymphs, has been the subtle companion of mermaids wherever they've gone. Even as belief in mermaids began to fade, the madness they inspired still thrived.

There was cause for celebration when the Fishmongers' Company of the City of London was granted the right to use mermaids in its coat of arms. Since at least 1293, The Worshipful Company of Fishmongers had been sponsoring pageants in London. As part of the spectacle, mermen and mermaids would parade through the streets; but in 1761, the fishmongers found a lasting place in the memory of Londoners by unleashing a flotilla of mermaids, hippocamps, dolphins, and a saint, who wove through the city on the waters of the Thames.

Mermaids were widely used on British tavern signs and occasionally were interpreted as a symbol of prostitution. The image of the dangerous half-animal seductress, hell-bent on dragging a man down, turned out to be exactly what many were seeking. The Mermaid Tavern in Cheapside (which was, in fact, owned by the fishmongers) became famous for the poets and writers who frequented it: Sir Walter Raleigh, William Shakespeare, Ben Jonson, Christopher Marlowe, and many others. Mermaids also became popular as a trademark of printing companies and were used inventively by paper makers as watermarks.

At the end of the Elizabethan era, in an age of rationalism, skepticism, and emerging commercial hubbub, mermaids retained a strong curiosity value. They were strange, alluring, and fun. Pondering the world's changing values and beliefs, the poet John Donne wrote:

> Go, and catch a falling star,
> Get with child a mandrake root,
> Tell me, where all times past are,
> Or who cleft the Devil's foot,
> Teach me to hear the mermaids singing.

As if certain individuals had misunderstood these lines as a literal challenge, bills advertising exhibits of "surprising fish or maremaids" were plastered about in European and American cities. These "mermaids" were on show in taverns, coffeehouses, and halls rented especially for the purpose, but their pedigree was somewhat suspicious.

In Spain, toward the end of the sixteenth century, an emaciated sailor who had been shipwrecked on an island and who had grown worn and wild-looking, was, with the help of makeup and tattoos, exhibited in a tub of water as a merman. But most of the mermaids exhibited were manmade creations known as Jenny Hannivers, assembled from parts of various animals.

The construction of these Jenny Hannivers approached the level of art among Japanese fishermen. The fisherman sewed the "mermaids" together or connected them in other ingenious ways so that no stitching or hardware was visible. The top half was usually a monkey, the bottom a fish. More ambitious examples incorporated wings and other flourishes. One, displayed at the Crown Tavern in London in 1738, included wings, feet, fins on the thighs, a tail, and even a head like a lion.

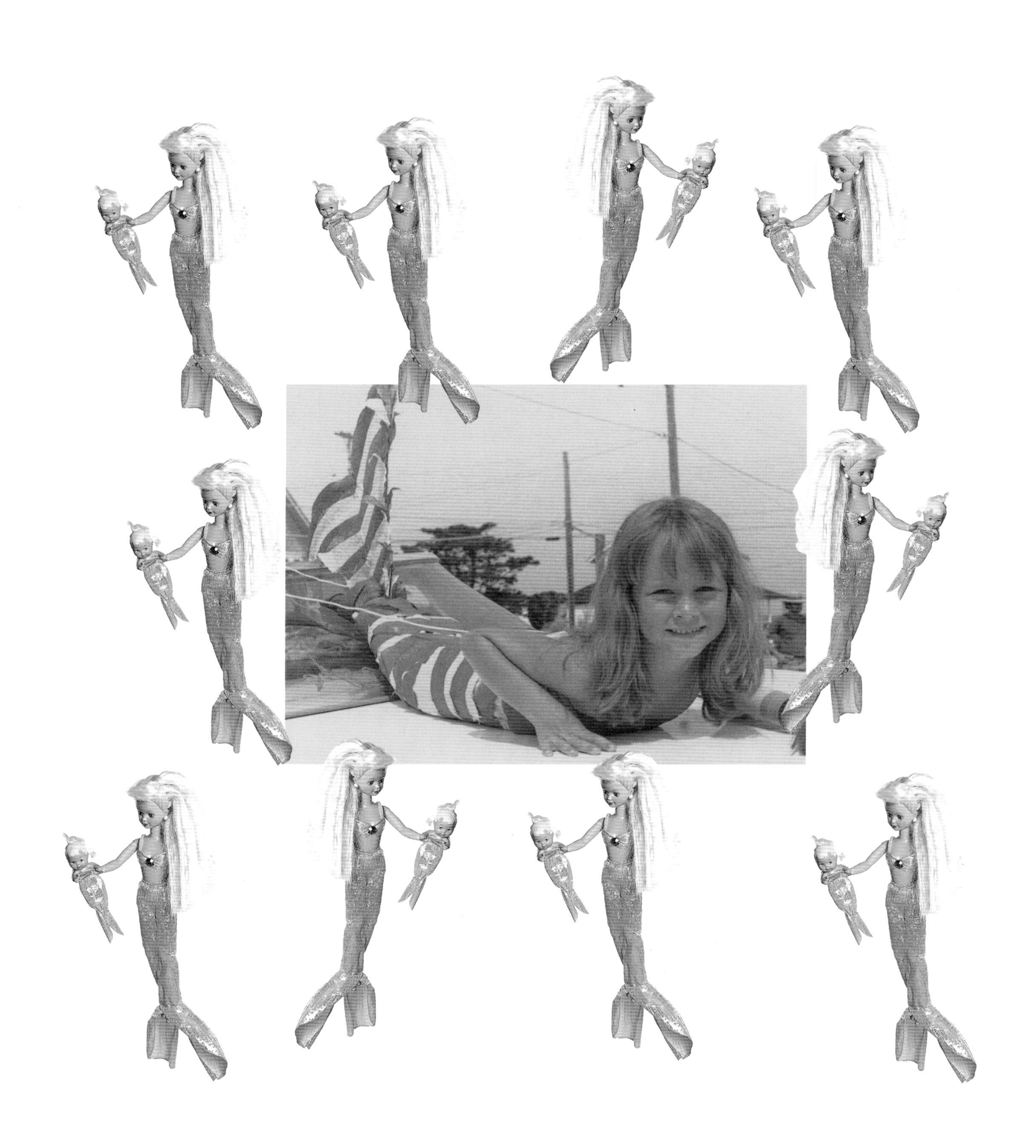

Wily fishermen would secretly assemble the "mermaid," then announce to the marketers that it had been caught. They would charge for the chance to see it and casually mention that before she died the mermaid predicted an epidemic that would affect anyone who did not protect themselves by wearing her image as a charm. Luckily, the fishermen happened to have some of these charms on hand to sell. As interest died out, fishermen would typically sell the creature to a traveler, who would take it to London or New York to exhibit.

The most famous example was the Fee Jee Mermaid, which was purchased for a large sum by an Englishman in India; it changed hands several times before it came into the possession of P. T. Barnum. Barnum exhibited the "mermaid" in New York, luring mobs who came expecting a beautiful mermaid and instead saw a grotesque amalgam of female orangutan and salmon.

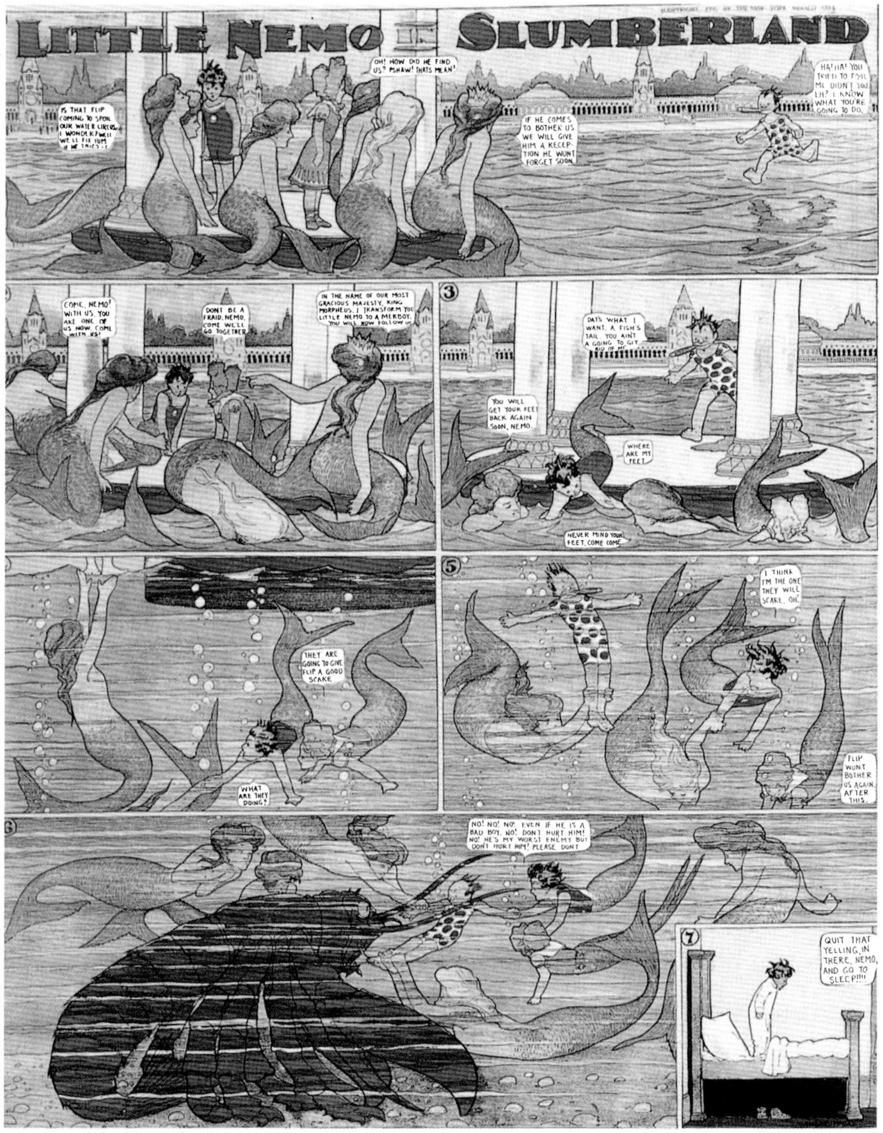

In 1822 the London papers reported that a man entered the office of the magistrates demanding protection for "himself, his mermaid, and his Sapient pig." The proprietor of an exhibition, the man had refused to admit two apparent hooligans. His suspicions were aroused because one of the men was in a "black silk gown and mustachios." When the proprietor suggested they come back the next morning, the two "raised a mob." Shouting, they threatened to return and to, in the proprietor's words, "blow up himself, barbeque his pig, and split his mermaid." The judge, apparently unimpressed, thought the proprietor should let the matter drop.

Today, amid the jangling hucksterism of Coney Island in New York, the old tradition of representing the mermaid as spirit of the place is preserved in the Annual Mermaid Parade. In a scene of indescribable madness, hundreds of people dressed as mermaids and mermen, from infant nymphs and Neptunes to old men and crones of the sea, march in a competition where the judges are openly bribed, mermaids weep in an attempt to sway the vote, and the natural order dissolves into its original chaos. At the parade's finish, King Neptune and the mermaid queen walk into the surf. In an echo of ancient fertility rites, Neptune plunges a giant thermometer into the Atlantic, turning up the ocean's temperature and marking the beginning of summer.

MERVEILLEUSEMENT GAZEUSE
Source
BRAULT
RIGOUREUSEMENT NATURELLE
Ph.H.Noyer 38
PUBLICITÉ
JOËL BELLON

Her Hair was a wet fleece of gold, and each separate hair as a thread of fine gold in a cup of glass. Her body was as white ivory, and her tail was of silver and pearl. Silver and pearl was her tail, and the green weeds of the sea coiled around it; and like sea-shells were her ears, and her lips were like sea-coral.

—Oscar Wilde, "The Fisherman and His Soul"

7¢ OFF
Surf

7¢ OFF
Surf
Surf
7¢ OFF

The work of Ralph Eugene Cahoon (1910–1982), an American painter who was born and spent his life on Cape Cod, Massachusetts, contains some of the most charming examples of art inspired by nympholepsy. Nearly every painting of his later career features at least one and more often several mermaids. Hardly the lachrymose mermaids of nineteenth-century genre painting, Cahoon's mermaids knit, play golf, paint, fish, hide in trees, ride bicycles, open Christmas presents, drink, have tea parties, help put out fires, pose for photographs, play games, and are generally up to every imaginable sort of high jinks. Painted in an almost naive style that is sly, humorous, and appealing, Cahoon's mermaids are an integrated part of the magic of everyday life.

Cahoon was far more than a master craftsman; his work was simple yet sophisticated, ordinary yet unique. His world—where mermaids and sailors flirt by the sea, where Julia Child makes bouillabaisse with the assistance of mermaids, and where hot-air balloons, lighthouses, and clipper ships are the stuff of daily life—was imaginative, colorful, and playful, and caught the attention of many important collectors, including Jacqueline Kennedy, who bought one of Cahoon's paintings for the president.

Ralph Cahoon lived a quiet life by the sea with his wife, Martha, also a painter. When he died, he left behind a treasure trove of paintings of his "buxom beauties." Much of Cahoon's work is in private collections, but the Cahoon Museum of American Art in Cotuit, Massachusetts, has a wonderful collection of this unique artist's enchanting work.

MEGANSETT
TEA
ROOM
1912
MEGANSETT

MERMAID INN
BOOKS
CHARTS

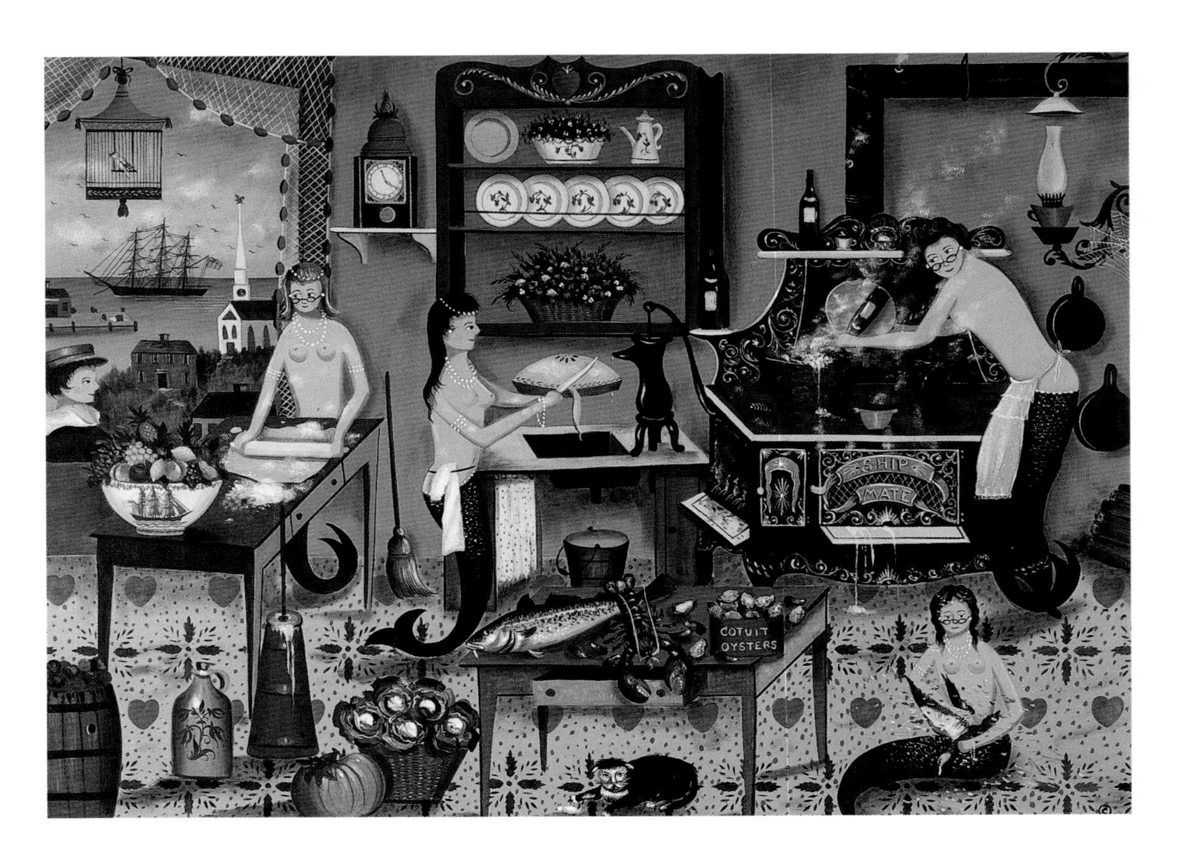
COTUIT
OYSTERS

the mermaid within

Toward the end of the nineteenth century, at a time when mermaids were rarely seen anymore, Sigmund Freud "discovered" the dark pools of the human unconscious. Concentrating on repressed sexuality, his work revealed an aspect of human instinct that resembled many of the traits expressed in stories about mermaids. For both Freud and his one-time associate Carl Jung, myths, legends, and ancient beliefs were not crude attempts to describe the world, but accurate descriptions of the inner workings of the human mind. The innocent-looking woman on the psychologist's couch might not have a fish tail, but she might nonetheless have all the traits of the most vicious Siren or carefree Nereid, and she might not even realize it. A man too, according to Jung, could have a mermaid within—a reflection of his feminine side that could be either cold or creative, depending on his attitude toward it.

In the 1930s, Jung became interested in the ancient art of alchemy. While alchemy's outward agenda was transmuting base metal into gold, Jung thought the alchemists' work was also a projection of inner workings reflecting a process of maturation and development within the human psyche. Mermaids appear in alchemical texts and engravings as guides leading the alchemist on his way. An engraving in one alchemical text shows two mermaids leading the alchemist. One leads him in the direction of a baby; the other leads to the city of God. In alchemy, the mermaid is a guide to the nature of the human mind, representing both what is human and what is animal and the necessity of reconciling the two into a coherent and lasting whole. The main difference between the alchemists and others is that the alchemists saw, believed in, and followed their mermaids—even when they led in two different directions. One alchemical text contains this motto: "Let nature be your guide; follow her with your art willingly, like a footman, For you will err if she is not your companion on your way." Jung's wife, Emma, wrote that as a symbol the mermaid wants to "entangle" us in "real relationships." She drags a man underwater not always to drown him, but sometimes to bathe him in the waters of life.

Mermaids are symbols—and who knows, maybe actual beings—that have been with us throughout history, reminding us of our relationship to the objective world, the rhythms of nature, the sound of water crashing on a beach, the way light moves across the surface of a wide bay, and the corresponding ripples of feeling they create within us.

Souls of Poets dead and gone,

What Elysium have ye known,

Happy field or mossy cavern,

Choicer than the Mermaid Tavern?

Have ye tippled drink more fine

Than mine host's Canary wine?

—John Keats, "The Mermaid Tavern"

TOPLESS SWIM SUITS
FORBIDDEN
ON THIS BEACH
PER ORDER * THE BREAKERS

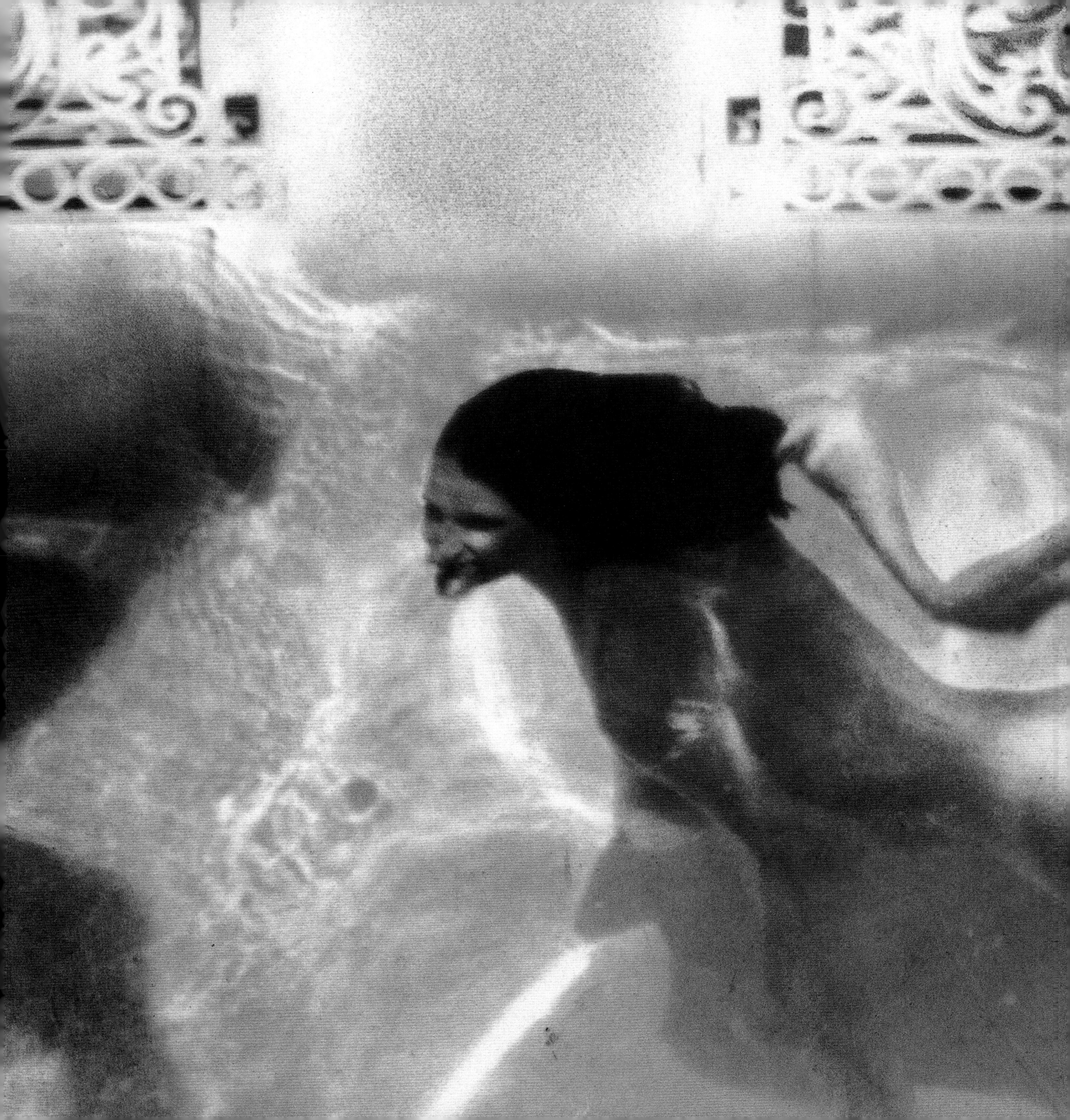

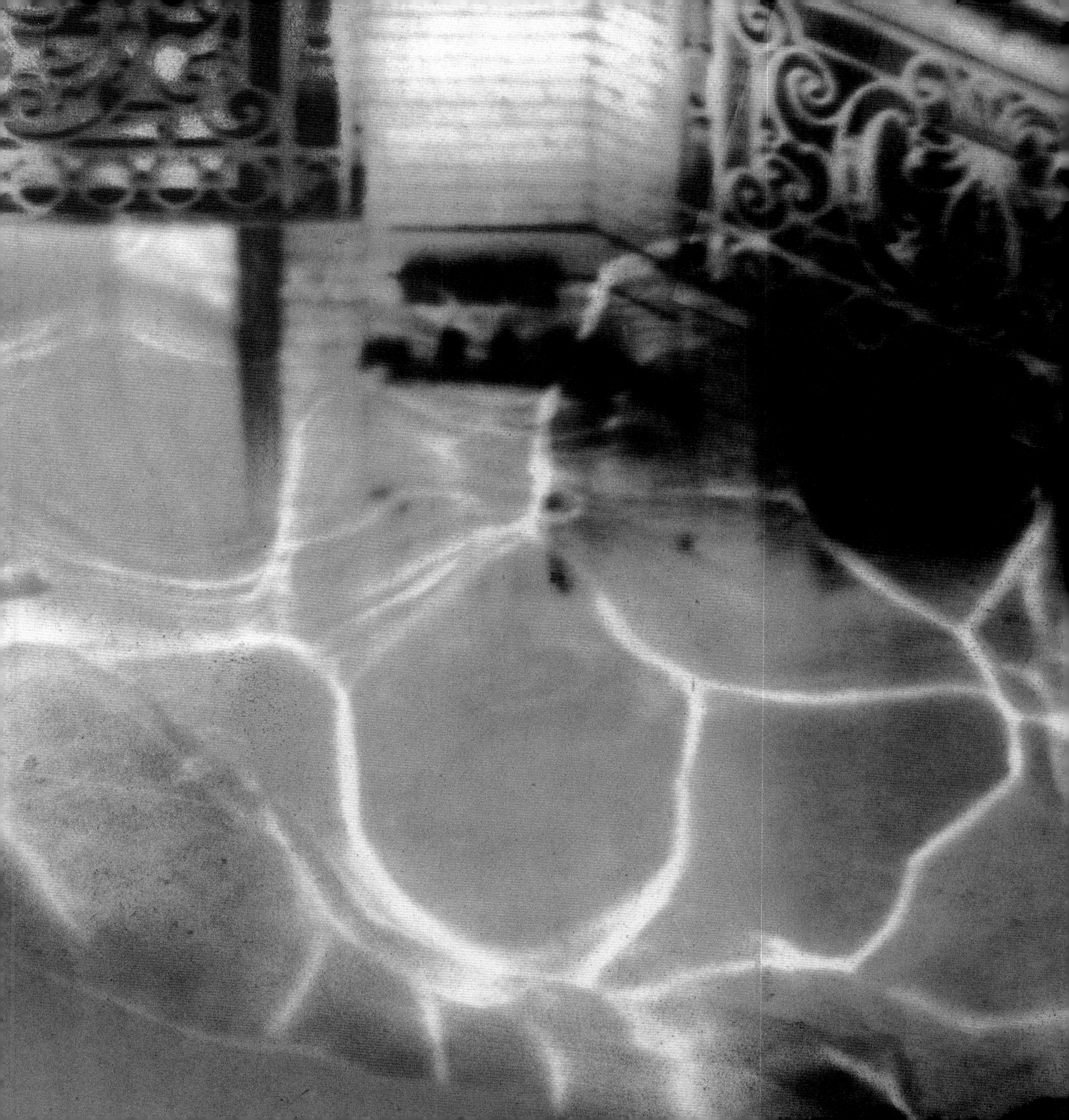

BIBLIOGRAPHY

Agosin, Marjorie. "Fish," *Women of Smoke*. Trans. Naomi Lindstrom and Ed. Yvette E. Miller. Pittsburgh, Pa.: Latin American Literary Review Press, 1988.

Apollonius of Rhodes. *The Voyage of Argo*. Trans. E.V. Rieu. London: Penguin Books, 1959.

Arnold, Matthew. "The Forsaken Merman," *A Sailor's Garland*. Selected and edited by John Masefield. Freeport, N.Y.: Books for Libraries Press, 1969.

Brown, William. "Song of the Syrens," *The New Oxford Book of Verse*. London: Oxford University Press, 1959.

Burton, Robert. *The Anatomy of Melancholy*. New York: Vintage Books, 1977.

Carrington, Richard. *Mermaids and Mastodons*. New York: Rinehart & Co., Inc., 1957.

Charbonneau-Lassay, Louis. *The Bestiary of Christ*. New York: Parabola Books, 1991.

Clair, Colin. *Unnatural History*. London, Toronto, and New York: Abelard-Schuman, 1967.

Craig, Robert D. *Dictionary of Polynesian Mythology*. Westport, Ct.: Greenwood Press, Inc., 1989.

Darley, George. "Song of the Mermaids," *Oxford Book of Nineteenth-Century English Verse*. New York: Oxford Press, 1964.

Dickinson, Emily. "I Started Early—Took My Dog—," *The Complete Poems of Emily Dickinson*. Ed. Thomas H. Johnson. Boston: Little, Brown and Company, 1960.

Donne, John. "Song (Go, and catch a falling star)," *The Complete Poetry and Selected Prose of John Donne*. Ed. with introduction by Charles M. Coffin. New York: Modern Library, 1994.

Ellis, Richard. *Monsters of the Sea*. New York: Alfred A. Knopf, 1994.

Eliot, T.S. "The Love Song of J. Alfred Prufrock," *The Complete Poems and Plays 1909–1950*. New York: Harcourt Brace Jovanovich, Publishers, 1980.

Evslin, Bernard. *The Sirens*. New York: Chelsea House Publishers, 1988.

Fabricius, Johannes. *Alchemy*. Wellingborough: The Aquarian Press, 1989.

Fraser, Sir James George. *The Golden Bough*. New York: Macmillan Publishing Co., 1922.

Freuchen, Peter. *Book of the Seven Seas*. New York: Julian Messner Inc., 1957.

Goethe, J.W. *Faust, Part Two*. London: Penguin Books, 1989.

Graves, Robert. *The Greek Myths*. London: Penguin Books, 1955.

——. *The White Goddess*. New York: The Noonday Press, 1969.

Gray, Louis. *Mythology of All Races*. 13 vols. New York: Cooper Square Publishers, 1964.

Haddawy, Husain, trans. *The Arabian Nights*. New York: Alfred A. Knopf, 1992.

Harding, Mary Esther. *Woman's Mysteries*. New York: G.P. Putnam's Sons, 1971.

Johnson, Buffie. *Lady of the Beasts*. Rochester, Vt.: Inner Traditions International, 1994.

Jung, Carl Gustav. *Aion*. Princeton, N.J.: Princeton University Press, 1963.

Jung, Emma. *Animus and Anima*. New York: Analytical Psychology Club of New York, 1957.

Keats, John. "The Mermaid Tavern," *John Keats*. Ed. Elizabeth Cook. Oxford and New York: Oxford University Press, 1994.

Lampedusa, Giuseppe di. "The Professor and the Mermaid," *Two Stories and a Memory*. Trans. Archibald Colquhoun. New York: Pantheon Books, 1961.

Lucretius. *On the Nature of the Universe*. London: Penguin Books, 1951.

Lum, Peter. *Fabulous Beasts*. New York: Pantheon Books, 1951.

Manley Hopkins, Gerard. "A Vision of the Mermaids," *The Cherry Tree: A Collection of Poems Chosen by Geoffrey Grigson*. New York: Phoenix House, 1959.

Manning-Sanders, Ruth. *A Book of Mermaids*. New York: E.P. Dutton & Co., Inc., 1968.

Marchant, R.A. *Beasts of Fact and Fable*. New York: Roy Publishers Inc., 1962.

Nietzsche, Friedrich. *Human All Too Human*. Cambridge and New York: Cambridge University Press, 1986.

Osborne, Mary Pope. *Mermaid Tales from Around the World*. New York: Scholastic Inc., 1993.

Pausanius. *Guide to Greece*. 2 vols. London: Penguin Books, 1971.

Phillpotts, Beatrice. *Mermaids*. New York: Ballantine Books, 1980.

Pliny the Elder. *Natural History*. London: Penguin Books, 1991.

Rilke, Rainer Maria. "The Third Elegy" and "II, 29," *Ahead of All Parting: The Selected Poetry and Prose of Rainer Maria Rilke*. Ed. and trans. Stephen Mitchell. New York: The Modern Library, 1995.

Shakespeare, William. *A Midsummer Night's Dream*. Ed. John F. Andrews. New York: Everyman's Classic Library, 1993.

Sheldrake, Rupert. *The Rebirth of Nature*. Rochester, Vt.: Park Street Press, 1994.

Snow, Edward Rowe. *Legends of the New England Coast*. New York: Dodd, Mead & Co., 1957.

Sweeney, James B. *A Pictorial History of Sea Monsters and Other Dangerous Marine Life*. New York: Crown Publishers, 1972.

Spenser, Edmund. "The Mermaids," *The Cherry Tree: A Collection of Poems Chosen by Geoffrey Grigson*. New York: Phoenix House, 1959.

Tennyson, Alfred, Lord. "The Mermaid," *Favorite Poems Old and New*. Ed. Helen Ferris. New York: Doubleday, 1957.

Thorndike, Joseph Jacobs, ed. *Mysteries of the Deep*. New York: American Heritage Publishing Co., Inc., 1980.

White, T.H. *The Book of Beasts*. New York: G.P. Putnam's Sons, 1954.

Wilde, Oscar. "The Fisherman and His Soul," *Oscar Wilde*. Ed. Isobel M. Murray. Oxford and New York: Oxford University Press, 1989.

Yeats, W.B. "The Mermaid," *The Collected Poems of W.B. Yeats*. Ed. Richard J. Finneran. New York: Collier Books, 1989.

SOURCES

MUSEUMS

The Cahoon Museum of American Art
4676 Falmouth Road
Box 1853
Cotuit, MA 02635
(508) 428-7581
Fax: (508) 420-3709

The Cleveland Museum of Art
11150 East Boulevard
Cleveland, OH 44106-1797
(216) 421-7340
Fax: (216) 421-1736

Delaware Art Museum
2301 Kentner Parkway
Wilmington, DE 19806
(303) 571-9590
Fax: (303) 571-0220

Independence Seaport Museum
Penn's Landing at
211 S. Columbus Boulevard & Walnut Street
Philadelphia, PA 19106-1415
(215) 925-5439

Kendall Whaling Museum
27 Everett Street
P.O. Box 297
Sharon, MA 02067
(617) 784-5642
Seventeenth-century natural histories
(Conrad Gessner, Penny Ambrose Penny)

Liverpool Museum
National Museums & Galleries on Merseyside
Walker Art Gallery
William Brown Street
Liverpool L3 8EL
United Kingdom
(151) 207-0001

Manchester City Art Galleries
City Art Galleries
Mosley Street
Manchester M2 3JL
United Kingdom
(161) 236-5244
Fax: (161) 236-2880

The Metropolitan Museum of Art
1000 Fifth Avenue
New York, NY 10028
(212) 535-7710

Musée de la Marine
Palais de Chaillot
75016 Paris
France
(1) 45-53-31-70

Musée du Louvre
34–36 Quai du Louvre
75058 Paris
France
(1) 40-20-50-50
Fax: (1) 40-20-54-52

Museo de Tapis
Plaza de España 17
San Ildefonso
Segovia, España 40100
(21) 470-019

Museum of American Folk Art
2 Lincoln Square
New York, NY 10023
(212) 496-2966

Mystic Seaport Museum
75 Greenmanville Avenue
P.O. Box 6000
Mystic, CT 06355-0990
(860) 572-5313
Fax: (860) 572-5371

Royal Academy of Arts
Piccadilly
London W1V 0DS
United Kingdom
(0171) 439-7438
Fax: (0171) 434-0837

Southampton City Council
City Art Services
Civic Centre
Southampton S014 7LP
United Kingdom
(0170) 322-3855
Fax: (0170) 383-2153

Victoria & Albert Museum
South Kensington
London SW7 2RL
United Kingdom
(0171) 938-8500

FOLK ART, GIFTS, DECORATIVES

Back from Guatemala: Andes to Himalayas
306 East Sixth Street
New York, NY 10003
(212) 260-7010
Hand-carved wooden mermaids, ornaments

Be Seated Inc.
66 Greenwich Avenue
New York, NY 10011
(212) 924-8444

Paul J. Bosco
Manhattan Art & Antique Center
1050 Second Avenue, Store #89
New York, NY 10022
(212) 758-2646
Fax: (212) 355-4403
Coins, medals, tokens, catalogs,
and occasional auctions

Chisholm Gallery
55 West 17th Street
New York, NY 10011
(212) 243-8834
Original vintage posters, turn-of-century through the fifties, with special emphasis on French twenties and thirties. Brault mermaids poster

Susan Daul Folk Art
624 Stratfordshire Drive
Matthews, NC 28105
(704) 847-6553
Folk art, fraktur

Dragon Tales
P.O. Box 8007
The Woodlands, TX 77387
(800) 848-3558
Mail order, greeting cards

Galerie Bourbon-Lally
23 rue Lamarre
Pétion-Ville, Haiti (W.I.)
(509) 57-6321
Fax: (509) 57-3974 or 57-3973

Little Rickie
49½ First Avenue (at Third Street)
New York, NY 10003
(212) 505-6467
Novelty folk art

The Magic Planter
The Cannery
2801 Leavenworth Street
San Francisco, CA 94133
(415) 775-1383
Various styles of planters, statuary, fountains, birdbaths available in various and custom finishes

Mood Indigo
181 Prince Street
New York, NY 10012
(212) 254-1176
Art deco accessories, original thirties through fifties dinnerware and collectables, novelty salt and pepper shakers

Museum of American Folk Art
Book and Gift Shop
2 Lincoln Square
New York, NY 10023
(212) 496-2966

Jerry Ohlinger's Movie Material Store, Inc.
242 West 14th Street
New York, NY 10011
(212) 989-0869
Fax: (212) 989-1660

Pacific Spirit
Whole Life Products
1334 Pacific Avenue
Forest Grove, OR 97116
(800) 634-9057
Fax: (503) 357-1669
Mail order, novelty gifts, mermaid mirror

Pardee Collection
P.O. Box 2926
Iowa City, IA 52244
(319) 337-2500

Récherché
171 Third Avenue
New York, NY 10003
(212) 979-1415
Novelty folk art

Rising Fawn Folk Art
714 Lindsay Street
Chattanooga, TN 37402
(615) 265-2760

Sailor's Valentine Gallery
40 Centre Street
Nantucket, MA 02554
(508) 228-2011

The Wright Collection Ltd.
168 Fifth Avenue
New York, NY 10010
(212) 229-0386
Woodcarvings, pewter figures, Christmas ornaments, folk art

CREDITS

Front Matter

Page 2: © Leah Demchick. **Page 6:** © Leah Demchick and Jürg Rehbein. **Page 9** inset: Courtesy of Weeki Wachee. **Page 9** border: © Mark Seelen; shakers courtesy Mood Indigo, New York, N.Y.

Introduction

Page 10: Paul Gauguin (1848–1903), *In the Waves (Ondine),* 1889. Oil on canvas, 92×72 cm. © The Cleveland Museum of Art, Gift of Mr. and Mrs. William Powell Jones, 78. 63. **Page 11**: © Leah Demchick and Jürg Rehbein. **Page 12**: *Mermaid of the S. Mariano Castle*. Archivi Alinari/Art Resource, N.Y. **Page 13**: *Dante and Virgil on Their Journey Underworld*—illumination for *The Inferno*, Canto XVII, Codex Urbanus Latinus 365. Biblioteca Apostolica Vaticana. **Page 14**: Raphael, *The Triumph of Galatea*, Palazzo della Farnesina, Rome. Scala/Art Resource, N.Y. **Page 15**: © Leah Demchick and Jürg Rehbein. **Page 17**: *Biblia Sacra Germanica* (Nuremberg Bible), Noah's Ark by courtesy of the board of trustees of the Victoria & Albert Museum. The Bridgeman Art Library. **Pages 18–19**: Ralph Eugene Cahoon, *Cape Knitting Company*. The Cahoon Museum of American Art. **Page 20**: Marc Chagall (1887–1985), *The Golden Age*. The Bridgeman Art Library. **Page 21**: Roman Mosaic (Third century A.D.), *Triumph of Neptune and Amphitrite*. Musée du Louvre, Paris.

The Sacred Fish

Page 22: *Hindu God Vishnu as a Fish*. Reproduced by the Permission of the British Library. **Page 23**: © Leah Demchick and Jürg Rehbein. **Page 24**: © Leah Demchick and Jürg Rehbein. **Page 25**: Courtesy Weeki Wachee. **Page 26**: © Leah Demchick and Jürg Rehbein. **Page 27**: © Mark Seelen; from the collection of Leah Demchick; object courtesy the Hatian Art Company, Key West, Fl. **Pages 28–29**: Hieronymus Bosch (1450–1516), *The Garden of Delights*, detail of center panel, top. Erich Lessing/Art Resource, N.Y. **Page 30**: © Leah Demchick. **Page 31**: background: Courtesy Arras.

Spirits of the Place

Page 32: Peter Paul Rubens (1577–1640), *Nereide and Triton*. Museum Boyams-Van Beuningen, Rotterdam. The Bridgeman Art Library. **Page 33**: © Leah Demchick and Jürg Rehbein. **Pages 34–35**: C.E. Boutibonne, *Sirènes*. EDIMEDIA. **Page 36**: © David Hughes. **Page 37** vellum: © Leah Demchick. **Page 37**: Copyright © 1996 by Universal City Studios, Inc. Courtesy of MCA publishing rights, a Division of MCA, Inc. All Rights Reserved. **Page 38**: Gustave Klimt (1862–1918), *Goldfish*. Solothurn Museum. **Page 38:** background: © Leah Demchick and Jürg Rehbein. **Page 39**: Alessandro Allori, *Fishing for Pearls*. Studiolo, Palazzo Vecchio, Florence, Italy. Scala/Art Resource, N.Y. **Pages 40–41**: Collier Smithers, *A Race with Mermaids and Tritons*. Whitford & Hughes, London. The Bridgeman Art Library.

The Sirens' Song

Page 42: Gustave Klimt (1862–1918), *Mermaids*, Zentralsparkasse-Bank, Vienna. The Bridgeman Art Library. **Page 43**: © Leah Demchick and Jürg Rehbein. **Page 44**: *A Mermaid and Her Mortal Lover*. Mary Evans Picture Library, London. **Page 45**: Musée de la Marine. **Page 46**: Herbert James Draper (1864–1920), *Ulysses and the Sirens*. Ferens Art Gallery, Hull. The Bridgeman Art Library. **Pages 48–49**: © Mark Seelen. **Page 50**: Peter Paul Rubens, *The Debarkation of Marie De'Medici in Marseilles*, detail of the Naiads. Musée du Louvre, Paris,

France. Giraudon/Art Resource, N.Y. **Pages 52–53**: Julius Olssen (1864–1942), *The Coast of the Sirens*. Phillips Fine Art Auctioneer/ EDIMEDIA.

Moon and Mirror

Page 54: Copyright © 1996 by Universal City Studios, Inc. Courtesy of MCA publishing rights, a Division of MCA, Inc. All Rights Reserved. **Page 55**: © Leah Demchick and Jürg Rehbein. **Page 56**: © Mark Seelen. **Page 57**: Luttrell Psalter (14th century). British Library. The Bridgeman Art Library. **Page 58**: © 1996 P. Delvaux Foundation-St. Idesbald/Belgium; licensed by VAGA, New York, N.Y. **Page 59**: © Mark Seelen; art courtesy W.Z. and D.E. Ginsberg. **Pages 60–61**: © Leah Demchick and Jürg Rehbein. **Pages 62–63**: *Nereid with Mirror*. Giraudon/Art Resource, N.Y.

The Mermaid's Soul

Page 64: © Leah Demchick. **Page 65**: © Leah Demchick and Jürg Rehbein. **Pages 66–67**: *Mermaids Accompanying the Ships from Le Roman de Sainte More*, 15th Century. Bibliothèque Nationale, Paris. The Bridgeman Art Library. **Page 69**: 12th-century mosaic. Erich Lessing/ Art Resource, N.Y. **Page 71**: *And Other Marine Creatures*. Mary Evans Picture Library. **Pages 72–73**: Gentile da Fabriano. *St. Nicholas Calms the Storm*. The Quaratesi polyptych. Pinacotea, Vatican Museums, Vatican. Scala/Art Resource.

The Seven Seas

Page 74: © Leah Demchick. **Page 75**: © Leah Demchick and Jürg Rehbein. **Page 76**: © Leah Demchick. **Page 77**: Jessie Marion King (1875–1949), *But Only a Little Mermaid Lying Fast Asleep*. Fine Art Photographic Library Ltd. **Pages 78–83**: © Leah Demchick and Jürg Rehbein. **Page 84**: Egnazio Danti (1536–1586), *A Raft of Cherubs*, from the Gallery of Maps (detail). Vatican Museums and Galleries, Rome. The Bridgeman Art Library. **Page 85**: Marc Chagall (1887–1985), *One Thousand and One Nights*. Kunstmuseum, Dusseldorf. The Bridgeman Art Library. **Page 86**: Courtesy Weeki Wachee. **Page 87**: inset: Ralph Eugene Cahoon, *Day's Catch*. The Cahoon Museum of American Art. **Page 87**: © Leah Demchick and Jürg Rehbein.

Romance and Magic

Page 88: Lord Frederick Leighton (1830–1896), *The Mermaid*. The City of Bristol Museum & Art Gallery. The Bridgeman Art Library. **Page 89**: © Leah Demchick and Jürg Rehbein. **Page 90**: © Leah Demchick and Jürg Rehbein. **Page 91** fortune-telling mermaid: ©HOTFOOT Studio. **Page 92**: "Married to a Mermaid," 1860s songsheet. The Bridgeman Art Library. **Page 93** background: © Leah Demchick and Jürg Rehbein. **Pages 94–95**: *Roman de Melusine*. EDIMEDIA. **Page 96**: John Archibald Woodside, Sr., *Advertisement for the Weccacoe Fire Engine Company*. Courtesy of the CIGNA Museum and Art Collection. **Page 97**: background: © Leah Demchick and Jürg Rehbein. **Page 98**: Ralph Eugene Cahoon, *Dancing by the Sea (Jullanar of the Sea)*. The Cahoon Museum of American Art. **Page 99**: Howard Pyle, *The Mermaid*. Delaware Art Museum, Howard Pyle Collection.

Sideshow

Page 100: Ralph Eugene Cahoon, *Sailor's Favorite*. The Cahoon Museum of American Art. **Page 101**: © Leah Demchick and Jürg Rehbein. **Page 102**: Courtesy Weeki Wachee. **Page 104** border: © Mark Seelen. **Page 103**: Packaged Goods Incorporated; art by Gene Wheeler. **Page 104** inset: Courtesy of Ames B. Massey. **Page 105**: © Mark Seelen. **Page 106**: *Little Nemo*. Collection of Richard Marshall. **Page 107**: © Mark Seelen; poster courtesy Chisholm Gallery, New York, N.Y. **Page 108**: © Mark Seelen. **Page 109**: tattoo: © HOTFOOT Studio. **Pages 110–111**: Ralph Eugene Cahoon, *Mermaid's Wash Day*. The Cahoon Museum of American Art. **Page 112** top: Ralph Eugene Cahoon, *True Grit*. The Cahoon Museum of American Art. **Page 112** bottom: Ralph Eugene Cahoon, *Balloons over Nantucket*. The Cahoon Museum of American Art. **Page 113** top left: Ralph Eugene Cahoon, *Megansett Tea Room*. The Cahoon Museum of American Art. **Page 113** top right: Ralph Eugene Cahoon, *The Rescue*, The Cahoon Museum of American Art. **Page 113** bottom left: Ralph Eugene Cahoon, *Fire at the Mermaid Inn*. The Cahoon Museum of American Art. **Page 113** bottom right: Ralph Eugene Cahoon, *Bon Appétit*. The Cahoon Museum of American Art.

The Mermaid Within

Page 114: Emile Jean Horace Vernet (1789–1863), *A Sea Nymph*. Christie's, London. The Bridgeman Art Library. **Page 115**: © Leah Demchick and Jürg Rehbein. **Page 116**: inset: Rene Magritte (1898–1967), *The Forbidden World*. The Bridgeman Art Library. **Pages 116–117**: © Leah Demchick. **Page 119**: Ralph Eugene Cahoon, *Topless Swimsuits Forbidden*. The Cahoon Museum of American Art. **Pages 120–121**: © Leah Demchick.

We have strived to obtain the necessary permission for reproduction of the illustrations contained within these pages and to provide the proper copyright credits. We would appreciate notification on any error of omission, which we will amend in all subsequent printings.

INDEX

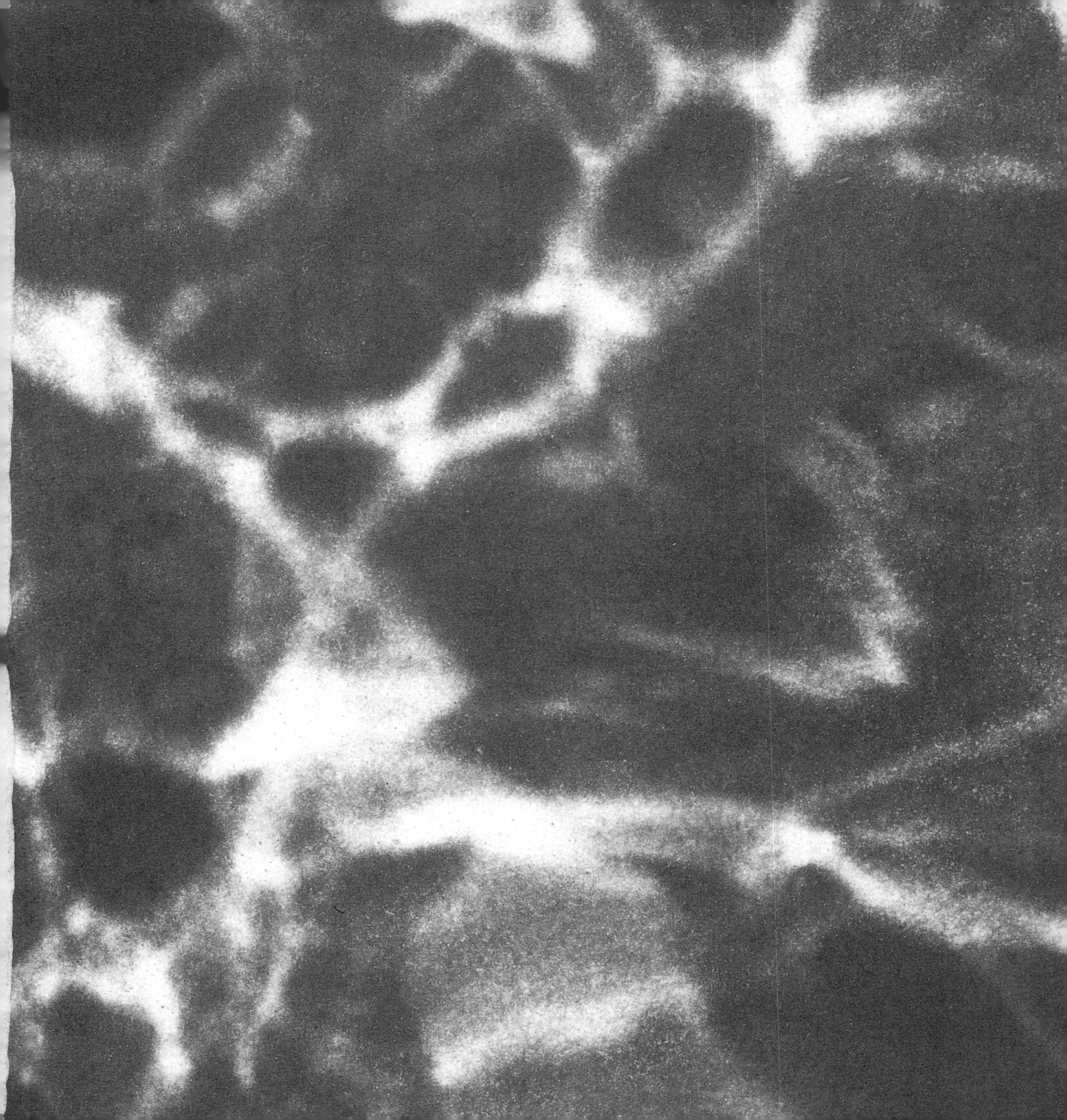

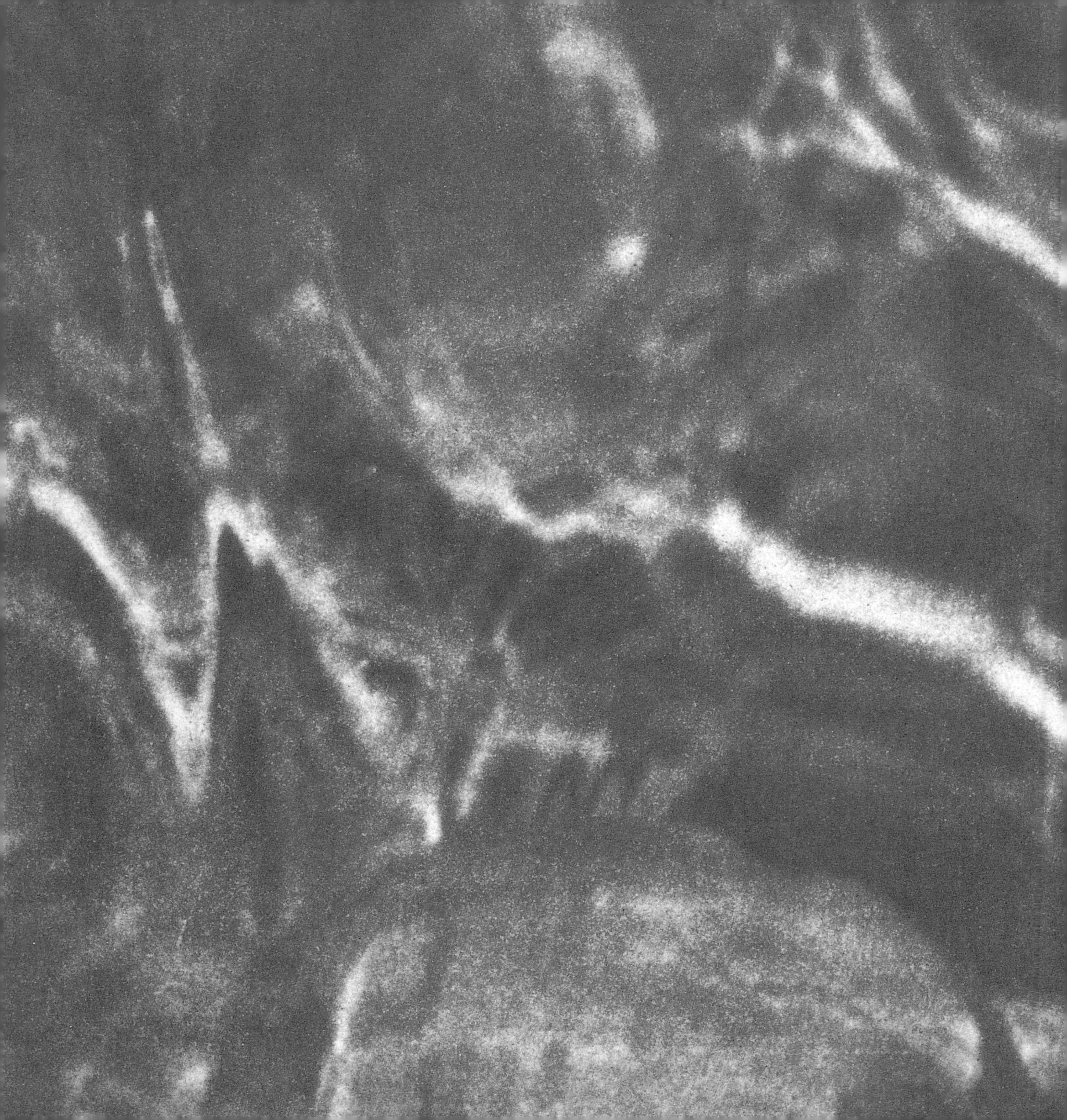